200 fasting-diet recipes

hamlyn | **all color cookbook**

200 fasting-diet recipes

An Hachette UK Company
www.hachette.co.uk

First published in Great Britain in 2014 by Hamlyn
a division of Octopus Publishing Group Ltd
Endeavour House, 189 Shaftesbury Avenue
London WC2H 8JY
www.octopusbooksusa.com

Copyright © Octopus Publishing Group Ltd 2014

Distributed in the US by Hachette Book Group USA,
1290 Avenue of the Americas, 4th and 5th Floors,
New York, NY 10020, USA

Distributed in Canada by Canadian Manda Group,
664 Annette St., Toronto, Ontario, Canada M6S 2C8

ISBN. 970-0-600 62083 2

Printed and bound in China.

1 2 3 4 5 6 7 8 9 10

Standard level kitchen spoon and cup measurements
are used in all recipes.

Ovens should be preheated to the specified temperature—
if using a convection oven, follow the manufacturer's
instructions for adjusting the time and temperature.

Fresh herbs should be used unless otherwise stated.
Large eggs should be used unless otherwise stated.
Freshly ground black pepper should be used unless
otherwise stated.

Some recipes are specified for those following a gluten-
free diet. It is prudent to check the labels of all prepared
ingredients for the inclusion of any ingredients that may
contain gluten, because different brands may vary.

This book includes dishes made with nuts and nut
derivatives. It is advisable for those with known allergic
reactions to nuts and nut derivatives or those who may
be potentially vulnerable to these allergies, such as
pregnant and nursing mothers, people with weakened
immune systems, the elderly, babies, and children, to
avoid dishes made with these. It is prudent to check the
labels of all prepared ingredients for the possible inclusion
of nut derivatives.

contents

introduction

introduction

If you've picked up this book, you may already be a convert to intermittent fasting. Alternatively, you may have heard about its benefits and are wondering whether to try it. At the other end of the scale, you may be a battle-weary diet skeptic, still holding out a small hope that you'll one day find the way to shape up and feel healthier permanently. Whatever your starting point or motivation, and whether you have a small or large amount of weight to lose or would just like to feel more comfortable in your own skin, this is the cookbook for you.

So what is the intermittent fasting approach to weight loss, and how does it work? There are any number of ways in which people practice intermittent fasting, from one day of light eating a week to no food at all for several days in a row. The approach works well for most people because it's a pragmatic solution that steers a safe, doable, and yet effective path through these extremes.

How to use this book

The plan allows normal eating for five days a week (including treats and meals out) and then restricts calorie intake to 500 calories a day for women and 600 calories a day for men (one-quarter of the normal recommended daily intake) for the other two days of the week. For most people, this is the perfect compromise that allows for socializing, family life, and work commitments, while still introducing enough calorie control to make sure that they lose weight at a healthy, steady rate.

With its delicious and innovative recipe selection, this book shows just how flexibly you can consume your 500 or 600 calories to keep the hunger wolf from the door and, yes, even tickle your taste buds at the same time. It also includes some sweet treats that are suitable for a fast day.

Ultimately, you'll be losing weight by eating, overall, fewer calories than your body

---

ABOUT THE RECIPES

All the recipes in this book are clearly marked with the number of calories (cal) per serving. These figures assume that you are using low-fat versions of dairy products, so be sure to use skim milk and low-fat yogurt. They have also been calculated using lean meat, so make sure you trim meat of all visible fat and remove the skin from chicken breasts. Don't forget to take note of the number of servings each recipe makes and divide up the quantity of food accordingly, so that you know just how many calories you are consuming.

You'll find ideas for accompaniments and alternatives to the main recipes throughout the book—these contain the same calories or up to 20 calories more than the main recipe. However, always be careful of any additional accompaniments you may be tempted to serve with a dish, because they can be deceiving and will all contribute to your total calorie consumption.

uses. However, where the diet is particularly great is how wonderfully achievable it can make this task for food lovers. People who find success, often report that they failed to lose weight in the past because cutting back every day was such a struggle, whereas doing so for just a couple of days a week, albeit more drastically, is a much more attractive proposition. Better still, far from being a short-term fad, those who practice intermittent fasting find it is a lifestyle choice that they can stick to because it doesn't take over their whole lives, doesn't demonize specific foods, and can even run alongside other supportive weight-loss programs, such as online food-diary methods.

So what about the health benefits of the diet? As you lose body fat and get thinner, you can expect to greatly reduce your chance of having a heart attack or developing heart disease. And, in strands of research unrelated to the weight-loss benefits, there's a growing ground swell of science that shows that periodically putting your body into a fasted state may cause various chemical changes linked with a lower risk of age-related diseases and a higher chance of living healthier for longer—see pages 10–13 for more details.

Whether you're in search of healthy food inspiration, or just intrigued to know more about intermittent fasting, you'll find something in this book for you. Read, digest, get thinner, and enjoy.

Is the diet for everyone?

Most overweight adults can benefit from this diet, but it should never be embarked on by children or adolescents, for whom any form of nutritional stress is undesirable. Also, do not adopt the diet if any of the following apply (check with your medical practitioner if you are uncertain):

- You are pregnant, trying to get pregnant, or breastfeeding.
- You are already at the bottom end of your healthy weight. You can check this using an online Body Mass Index (BMI) calculator— a BMI of 20 or less would indicate that you are not a candidate for this, or indeed any weight-loss program.
- You are an elite athlete or in training for a marathon or other big stamina event.
- You are diabetic.
- You have irritable bowel syndrome (IBS).
- You have been diagnosed with an eating disorder, either recently or in the past.

What is intermittent fasting?

People have fasted—out of choice or through necessity—for millennia, so the general concept is far from new. Fasting for physical well-being and spiritual reflection is as old as the hills and all of the big religions, such as Judaism, Buddhism, Christianity, and Islam, embrace fasting.

Interest was roused in the 1930s (and repeatedly since) when scientists found that restricting the calories fed to various animals and insects increased their lifespan. The idea of severely restricting calories every other day—instead of by a smaller amount every day—came later, in 2003, with laboratory research carried out at the National Institute on Aging (NIA). The concept of intermittent fasting for managing weight reached a mass audience when Dr. Michael Mosley presented the theories in a program in the British BBC TV documentary series *Horizon* that was aired in August 2012.

The health benefits

There is evidence to suggest that intermittent fasting may bring health benefits over and above those offered by a conventional calorie-controlled diet.

Weight loss

When you eat 500 or 600 calories for only two days a week and don't significantly overcompensate during the remaining five days (and evidence shows that most people don't), it stands to reason that weight will start to fall off. But research indicates that intermittent fasting may help people shed

excess weight in a more efficient and effective way than normal calorie restriction.

In particular, a 2011 review by researchers at the University of Illinois in Chicago found that people who did alternate day fasting (a repeating pattern of one day unrestricted eating followed by one day of no- or low-calorie fasting) were more likely to retain higher amounts of muscle tissue while losing at least as much fat. This is important because muscle helps to keep your metabolic rate higher, in essence because it is much more metabolically active than other tissues. In short, by having a more muscular frame, you can continue to burn more calories all day every day, even when you are sitting down or sleeping, which is very helpful in managing your weight over the longer term.

What doesn't kill you makes you stronger
According to Professor Mark Mattson, reported by *New Scientist* magazine to be the world's most cited neuroscientist, fasting is a type of hormesis—a process whereby organisms exposed to low levels of stress or toxins become more resistant to tougher challenges.

For example, the mild biological stress induced by fasting causes cells in the heart and digestive tract to produce proteins that decrease heart rate and blood pressure and increase digestive tract motility (the movement of food through the digestive tract), thereby reducing the risk of heart disease, stroke, and

colon cancer. It really does seem to be a case of what doesn't kill you (that is, managing on minimum food for a couple of days a week) makes you stronger!

Diabetes and blood sugar control
Any amount of weight loss in obese individuals, however it is achieved, will result in the body becoming more sensitive to insulin, which is an important step toward reducing the risk of diabetes—and exercise also has the effect of making you more responsive to insulin (see page 16). However, intermittent fasting could have a particularly good effect on your blood sugar control and diabetes risk.

In one of Dr. Michelle Harvie's studies for the UK charity Genesis Breast Cancer Prevention at Manchester's Wythenshawe Hospital, women who were on an intermittent-fasting style diet—consisting largely of milk and vegetables, adding up to 650 calories for two days each week—and a Mediterranean-style diet for the rest of the time, were compared with those who were restricted to 1,500 calories every day.

In both groups, women lost weight, reduced their cholesterol levels, recorded lower blood pressures, and had reduced markers of breast cancer risk. When it came to reductions in fasting insulin and insulin resistance—both signs that the diabetes risk has decreased—the benefits, although modest, were greater in the intermittent-fasting diet group than those using conventional calorie restriction.

Heart disease

As I have already alluded to, a reduction in cardiovascular risk factors, such as LDL cholesterol (that's the "bad" type that carries cholesterol toward the arteries, where it collects and causes "furring") and high blood pressure, can be expected on the diet. Triglycerides in the blood will also tend to fall as you lose weight—put simply, this means that your blood is less sticky and is, therefore, less liable to clot.

Much of the work in this area has been done by Dr. Krista Varady and her team at the University of Illinois in Chicago, with one of her scientific papers on the subject being entitled "Intermittent fasting combined with calorie restriction is effective for weight loss and cardio-protection in obese women" (November 2012). The research carried out by Dr. Varady outlines how intermittent fasting and wider, healthy weight loss can benefit heart health. Her findings are all very much in the paper's title.

Brain function

Much of the research into intermittent fasting actually started, and continues, in the healthy aging field, and brain aging in particular. At the National Institute on Aging (NIA), they've been investigating rats and mice that have been genetically engineered to develop Alzheimer's disease. Given normal circumstances, these animals show obvious signs of dementia by the time they are a year old (for example, becoming disorientated in a maze that they have previously been able to navigate with ease), but when they're put on an on/off fasting routine, they don't develop dementia until they're around 20 months old, or much nearer the natural end of their lives.

What could be the reason? One thing that's been reported is that the fasting mouse's brain produces more of a protein called BDNF (brain-derived neurotrophic factor), which stimulates the growth of new nerve cells in the hippocampus part of the brain, essential for learning and memory. There's certainly an evolutionary logic for the fasting state to be linked with better cognitive function, too; if you were hungry in caveman days, you needed your wits about you to track down the next meal and survive.

As yet there are still many unknowns, such as whether longer periods of fasting

are needed than normally experienced on an intermittent-fasting diet, and the human studies have still to be carried out, so it's impossible to say if intermittent fasting will help to prevent dementia. However, it's certainly a very interesting area of research.

Cancer

Much of the published research into the potential disease-protective effects of intermittent fasting involve measuring a biological marker called insulin-like growth factor 1 (IGF-1), which is known to be associated with cancer. Fasting has the effect of reducing IGF-1 levels, at least temporarily, and also seems to stimulate genes that repair our body's cells.

How a reduction in IGF-1 translates into successful real-world outcomes (such as a reduced chance of people getting cancer) is still unclear. One 2007 clinical review did look at "real-world" health outcomes and concluded that intermittent fasting (specifically, alternate day fasting, which usually has a minimum of 18-hour periods without food) may have a protective effect against cancer, as well as heart disease and diabetes. However, it concluded that "research is required to establish definitively the consequences," which is a fair reflection of the science as it currently stands. In summary, how effective intermittent fasting is against cancer relative to other healthy-eating or weight-loss programs is still to be clarified.

Getting started

Before you begin following your diet, you'll need to consider some basic options and make appropriate choices to suit you and your lifestyle.

Choose your fasting days

As a first step, you'll need to decide which days will work best for you as fasting days. This may evolve over time, or from week to week, according to your circumstances. As a general rule, however, you're more likely to stick to the routine if you can repeat the same two days every week, so try to choose days that you'll need to deviate from only infrequently. For example, don't pick a Tuesday if this is the day when a friend will probably invite you over for lunch, or a Friday if you're going to be tempted by a takeout after work. For obvious reasons, weekend days may not be such good fasting days either, but everyone's different and you should choose what works for you.

The gender divide
On a fasting day:
- If you're a man, you should have no more than 600 calories.
- If you're a woman, you should have no more than 500 calories.
- It is a fact that, even if a man and a woman weigh the same, the man will usually burn more calories than the woman, because he has a higher proportion of muscle.

Fast day meals
The second decision to make is how you will spread your 500 or 600 calories over the fasting day. Again, this is based on personal preference, usually honed through trial and error. A satisfying format for many people is to bookend their day with two meals: a 100–200-calorie breakfast and a 300-calorie dinner, for example, with the possibility of 100 calories or so for snacking or another small meal in between, if desired. Other people report that they are happier if they don't eat their first morsel until brunch or lunch, while still others (usually men, on anecdotal evidence) prefer saving up their calories for just one reasonable-size meal, either a lunch or an evening meal.

Six top tips for beginners
1 The day before your first fast, eat well and aim to go to bed feeling neither hungry nor overfull. Getting an early night is good preparation. Trying to stuff in as much food as late as possible so that you don't feel hungry tomorrow is not.

2 Do your eating homework so that you know how you are going to spend your 500 or 600 calories, and which meals you are going to spread them between. Use the recipes in this book as inspiration, and be sure that you are stocked up with the requisite ingredients.

3 Try to make your environment as devoid of food temptations as possible, which means making sure that a stray slice of pepperoni pizza isn't the first thing screaming, "eat me!" when you open the refrigerator door.

4 Arm yourself with some kind of calorie counter—use an online app or Web site.

5 Be aware that choosing a less busy day to start your fasting may not be the best approach. As long as you have your food choices preplanned, a day with plenty to keep you occupied may be better.

6 If you find your first fast too hard and have to give in, you've probably just chosen the wrong day. Don't despair and try again another time, but leave it a few days before doing so.

Fast day eating

Theoretically, you could have a large burger and endless cups of black coffee on a fast day and be within your calorie allowance, but this wouldn't be good for you. Instead, use your fasting day to make balanced and healthy choices, using the following guidelines:

- Eat five a day—fill up on fruit and vegetables
- Include dairy and beans
- Include lean protein
- Choose good-quality carbs
- Choose calorie-free drink options
- Don't estimate.

Perfect fast day proportions

- **Concentrate on fruit and vegetables** (steamed, broiled, stir-fried, or in soups, smoothie, and salads) as your primary stomach-filling priority (up to 200 calories).
- **Most of the remaining calories** (300 or 400) will be best spent on low-GI, carbohydrate-rich, and/or protein-rich foods.
- **Any leftover calories** you can use as you want (see below for ideas), but choosing more highly nutritious foods is preferable.

Give yourself a treat

- **Snacks up to 50 calories** include 6 cherry tomatoes, 1 oatcake cracker spread with yeast extract or an envelope of miso soup with tofu.
- **Snacks up to 100 calories** include 1 medium apple or banana, 2 tablespoons plain almonds, 1 plain cookie, or 1 hard-boiled egg.

"Off" day eating

Does all this mean you can truly eat anything you want to on your five free days? Well, yes, but there are limits. Studies consistently show that, contrary to what you might expect, intermittent fasters are actually very unlikely to go on big binges on their "off" days. Instead of making your appetite more extreme, the intermittent fasting seems to help naturally regulate it so that you enjoy only as much food as you need when you aren't fasting.

Exercise and the diet

An exercise program can definitely complement your weight-loss progress, and will provide many attendant health benefits, such as stronger bones and a healthier heart. But how should you negotiate exercise on a fast day? The old wisdom was that you should be well fueled prior to exercise, but the latest evidence suggests that modest activity in the fasted state is actually good for you. In particular, exercising in the fasted state means that the body has to use fat as its primary fuel,

which is good news for the disappearance of those love handles. Another benefit of exercising on an empty stomach appears to be that you'll build muscle more effectively when you do get around to eating in the post-exercise period.

In a nutshell, there's no reason why you shouldn't work out on your fast day, with the ideal being to exercise when you are feeling hungry, perhaps in the afternoon, and then to follow with one of your fast-day meals. However, common sense must come into play, and if you're new to exercise, it's best to ease yourself into physical activity on only nonfast days. There's also some suggestion that women are better doing weights on fasting days, while men can particularly benefit from cardio work. Listening to your body is essential, and always stop exercising immediately if you feel faint, dizzy, or light-headed.

How active should I be?

Official guidelines suggest that for optimum health benefits you should be physically active (at the level of brisk walking or gentle cycling, for example) for at least 30 minutes five times a week. If you're doing something more vigorous, such as running or playing a racquet sport, you can get away with 75 minutes, or three 25-minute sessions a week. On top of this, one or two 20-minute sessions with weights are also recommended to maintain muscle tone and lean tissue levels, particularly in the over 40s.

Intermittent fasting for life

For now, the consensus approach from most people doing this diet who have already reached their ideal weight and don't want to become any thinner is to switch to 500- or 600-calorie fasting just one day a week. A small study showed that people who had lost weight could keep it off by doing this; however, another approach, if you want to maintain a slightly firmer watch on your weight, would be to continue with two fast days a week, but let them creep up to, say, 700 calories.

Some people may find that they can manage by using intermittent fasting now and again (intermittent intermittent fasting), or to stop for longer periods or even altogether. These folks will be the ones who have become confident in their own eating intuition to keep them safe from weight gain. In short, they can now trust their inbuilt hunger and fullness mechanisms (that were, in fact, there all the time) to stay comfortably at their optimum weight.

Whatever your approach, remember that you should always obtain pleasure from your eating and your diet should never become a terrible chore. If you choose intermittent fasting as your ongoing method of optimizing health and weight, the recipes that follow should make that eminently possible, for as long as you choose.

breakfasts & brunches

fruity summer milk shake

Calories per serving **89**
Makes **two 10 fl oz glasses**
Preparation time **2 minutes**

1 ripe **peach**, halved, pitted,
  and chopped
5 oz (about 1 cup)
  strawberries
1¼ cups **raspberries**
1 cup **skim milk**
ice cubes

Put the peach in a blender or food processor with the strawberries and raspberries and blend to a smooth puree, scraping the mixture down from the sides of the bowl, if necessary.

Add the milk and blend the ingredients again until the mixture is smooth and frothy. Pour the milk shake over the ice cubes in 2 tall glasses.

For soy milk & mango shake, replace the peach, strawberries, and raspberries with ½ large ripe mango and the juice of 1 orange. Puree as above, then pour in 1 cup light soy milk, blend, and serve over ice cubes as above.

maple-glazed granola with fruit

Calories per serving **246**
Serves **6**
Preparation time **20 minutes**,
   plus cooling
Cooking time **7–10 minutes**

2 tablespoons **olive oil**
2 tablespoons **maple syrup**
⅓ cup **slivered almonds**
⅓ cup **pine nuts**
3 tablespoons **sunflower
   seeds**
¼ cup **rolled oats**
1¾ cups **low-fat plain yogurt**

Fruit salad
1 **mango**, pitted, peeled,
   and sliced
2 **kiwifruit**, peeled and sliced
1 small bunch of **red seedless
   grapes**, halved
grated zest and juice of 1 **lime**

Heat the oil in an ovenproof skillet with a metal handle, add the maple syrup and the nuts, seeds, and oats, and toss together.

Transfer the pan to a preheated oven, at 350°F, and cook for 5–8 minutes, stirring once and moving the brown edges to the center, until the granola mixture is evenly toasted.

Let the mixture cool, then pack it into a storage jar, seal, label, and consume within 10 days.

Make the fruit salad. Mix the fruits with the lime zest and juice, spoon the mixture into 6 dishes, and top with spoonfuls of plain yogurt and granola.

For berry compote, to serve with the granola instead of the fruit salad, place 1 cup each of raspberries, blackberries, and blueberries in a saucepan with the grated zest and juice of 1 lemon. Heat gently until the fruit has softened and the blueberries burst, then sweeten with 1 teaspoon honey. Serve with the granola and yogurt as above.

moroccan baked eggs

Calories per serving **170**
Serves **2**
Preparation time **10 minutes**
Cooking time **25–35 minutes**

1½ teaspoons **olive oil**
½ **onion**, chopped
1 **garlic clove**, sliced
½ teaspoon **ras el hanout**
pinch of **ground cinnamon**
½ teaspoon **ground coriander**
2¾ cups **cherry tomatoes**
2 tablespoons chopped
  cilantro
2 **eggs**
salt and **black pepper**

Heat the oil in a skillet, add the onion and garlic, and cook for 6–7 minutes, until softened and lightly golden. Stir in the spices and cook, stirring, for an additional 1 minute.

Add the tomatoes and season well with salt and black pepper, then simmer gently for 8–10 minutes.

Sprinkle with 1 tablespoon of the cilantro, then divide the tomato mixture between 2 individual ovenproof dishes. Break an egg into each dish.

Bake in a preheated oven, at 425°F, for 8–10 minutes, until the egg whites are set but the yolks are still slightly runny. Cook for another 2–3 minutes if you prefer the eggs to be cooked through. Serve sprinkled with the remaining cilantro.

For Mexican baked eggs, heat 1 tablespoon olive oil in a skillet, add 1 chopped onion and 1 cored, seeded, and chopped red bell pepper, and cook until softened. Add 2 crushed garlic cloves and ½ teaspoon chili powder and cook, stirring, for another 1 minute. Stir in 1 (14 oz) can diced tomatoes and simmer gently for 8–10 minutes, then add 1 tablespoon chopped cilantro. Divide between 2 individual ovenproof dishes and break an egg into each, then bake as above. Serve with 1 pitted, peeled, and sliced avocado, if liked.

cranberry muffins

Calories per muffin **172**
Makes **12**
Preparation time **10 minutes**
Cooking time **18–20 minutes**

2⅓ cups **all-purpose flour**
4 teaspoons **baking powder**
⅓ cup firmly packed **light brown sugar**
3 pieces of **preserved ginger** from a jar, finely chopped (about 1 cup)
⅔ cup **dried cranberries**
1 **egg**
1 cup **skim milk**
¼ cup **vegetable oil**

Line a 12-section muffin pan with paper muffin liners. Sift the flour and baking powder into a large bowl. Stir in the sugar, ginger, and cranberries until evenly distributed.

Beat together the egg, milk, and oil in a separate bowl, then add the liquid to the flour mixture. Using a large metal spoon, gently stir the liquid into the flour until only just combined. The batter should look craggy, with specks of flour still visible.

Divide the batter among the muffin liners, piling it up in the center. Bake in a preheated oven, at 400°F, for 18–20 minutes, until well risen and golden. Transfer to a wire rack and serve while still slightly warm.

For whole-wheat apricot & orange muffins, replace 1¼ cups all-purpose flour with 1¼ cups whole-wheat flour. Use ⅔ cup chopped dried apricots instead of the cranberries and omit the ginger. Fold the finely grated zest of 1 orange into the batter before baking.

breakfast cereal bars

Calories per bar **156**
Makes **16**
Preparation time **10 minutes**,
  plus cooling
Cooking time **35 minutes**

7 tablespoons **butter**,
  softened
2 tablespoons packed **light
  brown sugar**
2 tablespoons **light corn
  syrup**
1¼ cups **millet flakes**
¼ cup **quinoa**
⅓ cup **dried cherries** or
  cranberries
½ cup **golden raisins**
3 tablespoons **sunflower
  seeds**
2 tablespoons **sesame seeds**
2 tablespoons **flaxseed**
½ cup **unsweetened dried
  coconut**
2 **eggs**, lightly beaten

Grease an 11 x 8 inch shallow rectangular baking pan.
Beat together the butter, sugar, and syrup in a bowl
until creamy.

Add all the remaining ingredients and beat well until
combined. Turn into the prepared pan and level the
surface with the back of a spoon.

Bake in a preheated oven, at 350°F, for 35 minutes,
until deep golden. Let cool in the pan.

Turn out onto a wooden board and carefully cut into
16 bars using a serrated knife.

For tropical cereal bars, prepare the recipe as above,
replacing the dried cherries or cranberries with ⅓ cup
finely chopped dried pineapple and replacing the golden
raisins with ½ cup dried mango.

vanilla muffins

Calories per muffin **198**
Makes **12**
Preparation time **10 minutes**,
  plus cooling
Cooking time **25 minutes**

1 **vanilla bean**
1 cup **skim milk**
2⅓ cups **all-purpose flour**
1 tablespoon **baking powder**
⅔ cup **granulated sugar**
2 **eggs**
¼ cup **vegetable oil**
1 cup **low-fat plain yogurt**
confectioners' sugar, for
  dusting

Line a 12-section muffin pan with squares of wax paper. Split the vanilla bean lengthwise, using the tip of a sharp knife, and place in a small saucepan with ½ cup of the milk. Bring just to a boil, then remove from the heat and let cool slightly. Remove the vanilla bean from the pan and scoop out the seeds with a teaspoon. Stir them into the milk and discard the bean.

Sift the flour and baking powder into a large bowl, then stir in the sugar. In a separate bowl, beat together the eggs, vegetable oil, yogurt, vanilla milk, and remaining milk. Using a large metal spoon, gently stir the liquid into the flour until only just combined.

Spoon the batter into the muffin liners and bake in a preheated oven, at 400°F, for about 20 minutes, until well risen and golden. Transfer to a wire rack and dust with confectioners' sugar. Serve slightly warm.

For cinnamon muffins, steep the milk with vanilla as above, also adding 1 cinnamon stick. Let the milk cool completely before removing the cinnamon stick and vanilla bean. Make the muffin batter as above and spoon into the muffin liners. Combine 1 tablespoon granulated sugar and 1 teaspoon ground cinnamon and lightly sprinkle over the muffins, then bake as above.

light 'n' low crepes

Calories per serving **194**
Serves **4**
Preparation time **5 minutes**,
    plus standing
Cooking time **25 minutes**

1 cup **whole-wheat flour**
1 **egg**
1⅓ cups **skim milk**
1 teaspoon **vegetable oil**, plus
    a little extra for cooking

Topping
mixed fresh berries
½ cup **low-fat crème fraîche**
    or **Greek yogurt**

Sift the flour into a bowl, also adding the bran in the sifter to the flour in the bowl.

Beat together the egg, milk, and oil in a separate bowl, then slowly add to the flour. Stir the mixture until a smooth batter forms. Let stand for about 20 minutes, then stir again.

Heat a little oil in a nonstick skillet, or spray with an oil-water spray. When the oil is hot, add 2 tablespoons of the crepe batter and shake the skillet so that it spreads. Cook for 2 minutes, until the underside is lightly browned, then flip or turn the crepe over and cook the other side for a minute or so.

Keep the crepe warm in the oven while you cook the rest; you can stack one on top of the other as they are cooked. The batter should make 8 crepes in total. Serve 2 crepes per person topped with a handful of mixed fresh berries and a dollop of crème fraîche or yogurt.

For strawberry & lime crush, to serve with the crepes, blend the grated zest and juice of 1 lime with 5 oz (about 1 cup) strawberries and 2 teaspoons honey in a bowl until it forms a coarse puree. Adjust the sweetness to taste and serve with the crepes.

piperade with pastrami

Calories per serving **186**
Serves **6**
Preparation time **20 minutes**,
    plus cooling
Cooking time **25 minutes**

6 extra-large **eggs**
thyme sprigs, leaves removed,
    or large pinch of **dried
    thyme**, plus extra sprigs
    to garnish
1 tablespoon **olive oil**
4 oz **pastrami**, thinly sliced
salt and **black pepper**

Sofrito
3 small, yellow, red, and/or
    green **bell peppers**
1 tablespoon **olive oil**
1 **onion**, finely chopped
2 **garlic cloves**, crushed
4 **tomatoes**, skinned (see
    page 162), seeded and
    chopped

Make the sofrito. Broil or cook the bell peppers directly in a gas flame for about 10 minutes, turning them until the skins have blistered and blackened. Remove the bell peppers and place them in a plastic bag. Seal and let cool for 20 minutes, then rub the skins from the flesh and discard. Rinse the bell peppers under cold running water. Halve and seed, then cut the flesh into strips.

Heat the oil in a large skillet, add the onion, and cook gently for 10 minutes, until softened and transparent. Add the garlic, tomatoes, and bell peppers and simmer for 5 minutes, until any juice has evaporated from the tomatoes. Set aside until ready to serve.

Beat the eggs with the thyme and salt and black pepper in a bowl. Reheat the sofrito. Heat the oil in a saucepan, add the eggs, stirring until they are lightly scrambled. Stir into the reheated sofrito and spoon onto 6 plates.

Arrange slices of pastrami around the eggs and serve immediately, garnished with a little extra thyme.

For poached egg piperade, make the sofrito as above. Place 1 (10 oz) package washed baby spinach leaves in a large saucepan, cover, and cook briefly just until the leaves start to wilt. Divide among 6 serving plates, then spoon the sofrito over the top. Poach the 6 eggs (see page 106) instead of scrambling them, then sit them on top. Dust each egg with a tiny pinch of paprika and serve, omitting the pastrami.

corn & bacon muffins

Calories per muffin **228**
Makes **12**
Preparation time **10 minutes**
Cooking time **20–25 minutes**

6 **bacon slices**, excess fat
   removed, finely chopped
1 small **red onion**, finely
   chopped
1 ⅓ cups **frozen corn kernels**
1 ¼ cups **fine cornmeal**
1 cup **all-purpose flour**
2 teaspoons **baking powder**
⅓ cup shredded **cheddar
   cheese**
1 cup **skim milk**
2 **eggs**
3 tablespoons **vegetable oil**

Lightly oil a 12-section muffin pan.

Dry-fry the bacon and onion in a nonstick skillet over medium heat for 3–4 minutes, until the bacon is turning crisp. Meanwhile, cook the corn in a saucepan of boiling water for 2 minutes to soften. Drain.

Put the cornmeal, flour, and baking powder into a bowl and mix together. Add the corn, cheese, bacon, and onions, then stir in.

Whisk the milk with the eggs and oil in a separate bowl, then add to the dry ingredients. Stir gently until just combined, then divide the batter among the muffin pan sections.

Bake in a preheated oven, at 425°F, for 15–20 minutes, until golden and just firm. Loosen the edges of the muffins with a knife and transfer to a wire rack to cool.

For spiced corn & scallion muffins, omit the bacon. Prepare the recipe as above, replacing the red onion with 4 scallions, sliced thinly into circles. Add 1 teaspoon hot paprika and 1 seeded and finely chopped red chile to the batter before baking as above.

potato drop pancakes

Calories per scone **68**
Makes **12**
Preparation time **10 minutes**,
   plus cooling
Cooking time **20–25 minutes**

4 large **russet potatoes**,
   peeled and cut into small
   chunks
1½ teaspoons **baking powder**
2 **eggs**
⅓ cup **skim milk**
vegetable oil, for frying
salt and **black pepper**

Cook the potatoes in a saucepan of lightly salted boiling water for 15 minutes or until completely tender. Drain well, return to the saucepan, and mash until smooth. Let cool slightly.

Beat in the baking powder, then the eggs, milk, and a little seasoning, and continue to beat until everything is evenly combined.

Heat a little oil in a heavy skillet. Drop tablespoonfuls of the batter into the pan, spacing them slightly apart, and cook for 3–4 minutes, turning once, until golden.

Transfer to a serving plate and keep warm while cooking the remainder of the potato batter to make 12 pancakes. (If broiling the potato pancakes, put 12 tablespoonfuls of the batter onto an oiled, aluminum foil-lined baking sheet and cook under a preheated broiler for 5 minutes, turning once halfway through the cooking time.) Serve warm, drizzled with maple syrup and accompanied by broiled tomatoes and lean bacon slices, if liked (remembering to count the extra calories).

For mustard potato & green bean drop pancakes, prepare the mixture as above, adding ¾ cup finely sliced, blanched green beans and 1 tablespoon whole-grain mustard before cooking as above.

asparagus with smoked salmon

Calories per serving **150**
Serves **6**
Preparation time **10 minutes**
Cooking time **6 minutes**

18 trimmed thin **asparagus
  spears**
3 tablespoons coarsely
  chopped **hazelnuts**
4 teaspoons **olive oil**
juice of **1 lime**
1 teaspoon **Dijon mustard**
12 **quail eggs**
8 oz **smoked salmon**
salt and **black pepper**

Put the asparagus spears in a steamer, cover, and cook for 5 minutes, until just tender.

Meanwhile, broil the nuts on a piece of aluminum foil until lightly browned. Lightly mix together the oil, lime juice, and mustard with a little salt and black pepper in a bowl, then stir in the hot nuts. Keep warm.

Pour water into a saucepan to a depth of 1½ inches and bring it to a boil. Lower the eggs into the water with a slotted spoon and cook for 1 minute. Take the pan off the heat and let the eggs stand for 1 minute. Drain the eggs, rinse with cold water, and drain again.

Tear the salmon into strips and divide it among 6 serving plates, folding and twisting the strips attractively. Tuck the just-cooked asparagus into the salmon, halve the quail eggs, leaving the shells on if liked, and arrange on top. Drizzle with the warm nut dressing and serve sprinkled with a little black pepper.

For asparagus with prosciutto & ricotta, steam the asparagus and make the dressing as above. Remove the fat from 12 slices of prosciutto, then divide the slices among 6 plates, so each has 2 slices, and spoon 2 tablespoons ricotta into the center of each plate. Arrange the asparagus around the ricotta and drizzle with the dressing. Omit the quail eggs and smoked salmon.

zucchini & stilton fritters

Calories per fritter **95**
Makes **20**
Preparation time **10 minutes**
Cooking time **10 minutes**

1 tablespoon **olive oil**
1 large **zucchini**, chopped
3 **eggs**
⅔ cup **skim milk**
1¼ cups **all-purpose flour**,
  sifted
1 teaspoon **baking powder**
1 (15 oz) can **great Northern
  beans**, drained and rinsed
handful of **parsley**, chopped
3 **scallions**, sliced
1 (11 oz) can **corn kernels**,
  drained
¾ cup crumbled **Stilton** or
  other **blue cheese**

Heat a little of the oil in a nonstick skillet, add the zucchini, and cook for 3–4 minutes, until golden and tender.

Beat together the eggs, milk, flour, and baking powder in a bowl, then stir in the beans, parsley, scallions, corn, Stilton, and the cooked zucchini.

Heat the remaining oil in a nonstick skillet and add tablespoons of the mixture to the pan. Gently flatten each fritter with the back of a fork and cook for 1–2 minutes on each side, until golden. Repeat with the remaining mixture to make 20 fritters, keeping the fritters warm in a low oven.

Serve with tomato salsa, if desired (remembering to count the extra calories).

For spinach & Stilton fritters, replace the zucchini with 7 cups baby spinach leaves. Cook in a nonstick skillet with a little oil for 1–2 minutes, until wilted, then stir in the remaining ingredients, replacing the great Northern beans with 1 (15 oz) can of cannellini beans, and also adding a large pinch of freshly grated nutmeg. Cook and serve as above.

olive & sun-dried tomato biscuits

Calories per scone **198**
Makes **8**
Preparation time **15 minutes**
Cooking time **12 minutes**

1 cup **rice flour**
⅔ cup **potato flour**
1 teaspoon **xanthan gum**
1 teaspoon **baking powder**
1 teaspoon **baking soda**
6 tablespoons **butter**, cubed
¼ cup **pitted green olives**,
　chopped
4 **sun-dried tomatoes**,
　chopped
1 tablespoon chopped **parsley**
1 extra-large **egg**, beaten
¼ cup **buttermilk**, plus a little
　extra for brushing

Place the flours, xanthan gum, baking powder, baking soda, and butter in a food processor and blend until the mixture resembles fine bread crumbs, or rub in by hand in a large bowl.

Stir the olives, tomatoes, and parsley into the mixture, then, using the blade of a knife, stir in the egg and buttermilk until the dough comes together.

Turn the dough out onto a surface dusted lightly with flour and gently press it down to a thickness of 1 inch. Use a 2 inch cutter to cut out 8 biscuits.

Place on a lightly floured baking sheet, brush with a little buttermilk, and bake in a preheated oven, at 425°F, for about 12 minutes, until golden and risen. Transfer to a wire rack to cool.

For ham & cheese biscuits, prepare the dough as above, replacing the green olives with 1 oz coarsely chopped honey roast ham. Add 2 tablespoons grated Parmesan cheese to the mixture before working in the egg and buttermilk. Continue as above.

light lunches

lentil & pea soup

Calories per serving **141**
Serves **4**
Preparation time **10 minutes**
Cooking time **2 hours**

1 teaspoon **olive oil**
1 **leek**, trimmed and finely sliced
1 **garlic clove**, crushed
1 (15 oz) can **green lentils**,
   drained, or 2 cups cooked
   dried green lentils
2 tablespoons chopped
   mixed herbs, such as thyme
   and parsley
1⅓ cups **frozen peas**
2 tablespoons **low-fat crème
   fraîche** or **Greek yogurt**
1 tablespoon chopped **mint**
black pepper

Vegetable stock
1 tablespoon **olive oil**
1 **onion**, chopped
1 **carrot**, chopped
4 **celery sticks**, chopped
any **vegetable scraps**, such
   as celery tops, onion skins,
   and tomato skins
1 **bouquet garni**
5½ cups **water**
salt and **black pepper**

Make the stock. Heat the oil in a large saucepan, add the vegetables, and cook for 2–3 minutes, then add the vegetable scraps and bouquet garni and season well. Pour in the measured water and bring to a boil, then reduce the heat and simmer gently for 1½ hours, by which time the stock should have reduced to 3¾ cups. Drain over a bowl, discarding the vegetables and retaining the stock.

Heat the oil in a medium saucepan, add the leek and garlic, and sauté over gentle heat for 5–6 minutes, until the leek is softened.

Add the lentils, stock, and herbs and bring to a boil, then reduce the heat and simmer for 10 minutes. Add the peas and cook for another 5 minutes, until tender.

Transfer half the soup to a blender or food processor and blend until smooth. Return to the pan, stir to combine with the unblended soup, then heat through and season with plenty of black pepper.

Ladle the soup into 4 bowls. Stir together the crème fraîche or Greek yogurt and mint and serve alongside each bowl of soup.

For curried lentil & parsnip soup, make the stock as above. Heat the olive oil in a saucepan, add the leek and garlic with 2 chopped parsnips, and cook for 5–6 minutes, until the vegetables are softened. Add 1 teaspoon curry powder and cook, stirring, for 1 minute. Continue as above, omitting the peas.

chilled gazpacho

Calories per serving **135**
Serves **6**
Preparation time **20 minutes**,
    plus chilling

7 **tomatoes**, skinned (see
    page 162) and coarsely
    chopped
½ **cucumber**, coarsely
    chopped
2 **red bell peppers**, cored,
    seeded, and coarsely
    chopped
1 **celery stick**, chopped
2 **garlic cloves**, chopped
½ **red chile**, seeded
    and sliced
small handful of **cilantro** or
    flat leaf parsley, plus extra
    to garnish
2 tablespoons **white wine
    vinegar**
2 tablespoons **tomato paste**
¼ cup **olive oil**
salt

To serve
ice cubes
hard-boiled egg, finely
    chopped
cucumber, black pepper, and
    onion, finely chopped

Mix together the vegetables, garlic, chile, and cilantro or parsley in a large bowl.

Add the vinegar, tomato paste, oil, and a little salt. Process in batches in a food processor or blender until smooth, scraping the mixture down from the sides of the bowl, if necessary.

Collect the blended mixtures together in a clean bowl and check the seasoning, adding a little more salt, if needed. Chill for up to 24 hours before serving.

Ladle the gazpacho into 6 large bowls, sprinkle with ice cubes, and garnish with chopped parsley or cilantro and a little chopped hard-boiled egg, cucumber, black pepper, and onion. Serve with crackers, if desired (remembering to count the extra calories).

For chilled couscous gazpacho, prepare the soup as above, omitting the red bell peppers, and chill. Place ¼ cup couscous in a bowl and pour in just enough boiling water to come ½ inch above the level of the couscous. Cover with plastic wrap and set aside for 10 minutes. Uncover, break the couscous up with a fork, and let cool to room temperature. Stir into the soup just before serving with the chopped herbs and a little harissa on the side. Omit the ice and garnishes.

sweet potato & cabbage soup

Calories per serving **160**
Serves **4**
Preparation time **15 minutes**
Cooking time **25 minutes**

2 **onions**, chopped
2 **garlic cloves**, sliced
4 **bacon slices**, chopped
3 **sweet potatoes**, peeled
  and chopped
2 **parsnips**, peeled and
  chopped
1 teaspoon chopped **thyme**
3¾ cups **Vegetable Stock**
  (see page 48)
1 **baby savoy cabbage**,
  shredded

Place the onions, garlic, and bacon in a large saucepan and sauté for 2–3 minutes.

Add the sweet potatoes, parsnips, thyme, and stock and bring to a boil, then reduce the heat and simmer for 15 minutes.

Transfer two-thirds of the soup to a blender or food processor and blend until smooth. Return the soup to the pan, add the cabbage, and simmer for another 5–7 minutes, until the cabbage is just cooked.

Ladle the soup into 4 bowls and serve immediately.

For squash & broccoli soup, make the recipe as above, replacing the sweet potatoes with 3 cups peeled, seeded, and chopped butternut squash. After returning the blended soup to the pan, add 1½ cups small broccoli florets. Cook as above, omitting the cabbage.

bacon & white bean soup

Calories per serving **136**
Serves **4**
Preparation time **5 minutes**
Cooking time **15 minutes**

1 teaspoon **olive oil**
2 **smoked bacon slices**,
  chopped
2 **garlic cloves**, crushed
1 **onion**, chopped
a few **thyme** or **lemon
  thyme sprigs**
2 (15 oz) cans **cannellini
  beans**, drained and rinsed
3¾ cups **Vegetable Stock**
  (see page 48)
2 tablespoons chopped
  parsley
black pepper

Heat the oil in a large saucepan, add the bacon, garlic, and onion, and sauté for 3–4 minutes, until the bacon is beginning to brown and the onion to soften.

Add the thyme and cook for another 1 minute. Add the beans and stock to the pan and bring to a boil, then reduce the heat and simmer for 10 minutes.

Transfer the soup to a blender or food processor and blend with the parsley and black pepper until smooth.

Return the soup to the pan and heat through, then ladle into 4 bowls and serve immediately.

For herb & white bean crostini, lightly mash 1 drained (15 oz) can cannellini beans and then combine with 2 tablespoons each of finely chopped basil and parsley, 1 crushed garlic clove, a pinch of dried red pepper flakes, and 4 chopped cherry tomatoes. Toast 8 thin slices of baguette and top with the bean mixture.

miso broth with shrimp

Calories per serving **57**
Serves **6**
Preparation time **10 minutes**
Cooking time **12–13 minutes**

4 **scallions** or **baby leeks**,
  thinly sliced
¾ inch piece of **fresh ginger
  root**, peeled and finely
  chopped
½–1 large **red chile**, seeded
  and thinly sliced
6⅓ cups **fish stock** or
  Vegetable Stock
  (see page 48)
3 tablespoons **chilled miso**
2 tablespoons **mirin**
  (Japanese cooking wine)
1 tablespoon **soy sauce**
1½ cups thinly sliced
  bok choy
2 tablespoons chopped
  cilantro
5 oz **frozen cooked, peeled
  shrimp**, thawed and rinsed

Put the white parts of the scallions or leeks into
a saucepan with the ginger, sliced chile, and stock.

Add the miso, mirin, and soy sauce, stir, and bring to a
boil, then reduce the heat and simmer for 5 minutes.

Stir in the green parts of the scallions or leeks, the bok
choy, cilantro, and shrimp and cook for 2–3 minutes or
until the bok choy has just wilted. Ladle into 6 bowls
and serve.

For vegetarian miso broth, prepare the soup as above.
When adding the bok choy, also stir in 1 large carrot,
cut into matchsticks, and ½ cup bean sprouts. Cook as
above for 2–3 minutes. Omit the shrimp.

sautéed kidneys with red wine

Calories per serving **303**
Serves **6**
Preparation time **20 minutes**
Cooking time **20–25 minutes**

1 tablespoon **butter**
1 tablespoon **olive oil**
1 **onion**, thinly sliced
10 **kidneys**, cored and
   trimmed
2½ cups halved **cherry
   tomatoes**
1 teaspoon **Dijon mustard**
1 teaspoon **tomato paste**
1 cup **medium red wine**
8 **bacon slices**, excess fat
   removed
2 cups **arugula leaves**
4 teaspoons **balsamic vinegar**
3 slices of **whole-grain bread**
salt and **black pepper**

Heat the butter and oil in a skillet, add the onion, and sauté for 5 minutes, until softened and lightly browned. Add the kidneys and sauté over high heat for 3 minutes, until browned.

Add the tomatoes and cook for 2 minutes, then stir in the mustard, tomato paste, red wine, and salt and black pepper. Cook for 2–3 minutes, stirring, until the sauce has reduced slightly and the kidneys are cooked. Cover with a lid and keep hot.

Meanwhile, wind the bacon around 8 metal skewers and cook under a preheated hot broiler for 8–10 minutes, until crisp. Toss the arugula leaves in the vinegar. Toast the bread and cut each slice in half.

Arrange the toast on 6 serving plates and spoon the the kidneys onto the toast. Slide the skewers from the bacon and arrange the bacon attractively on the kidneys. Spoon the arugula salad on the side and serve immediately.

For beef strips with red wine, replace the kidneys with 1 lb lean sirloin steak, cut into thin strips. Cook the beef with the ingredients up to and including the red wine as above, then remove from the heat and stir in the arugula, balsamic vinegar, and ⅓ cup toasted pine nuts. Set aside for the arugula to wilt. Omit the bacon and toast, and serve.

peppered beef with salad greens

Calories per serving **148**
Serves **6**
Preparation time **20 minutes**
Cooking time **4–7 minutes**

2 **thick-cut tenderloin steaks**
   (about 1 lb in total), trimmed
   of fat
3 teaspoons **colored**
   peppercorns, coarsely
   crushed
coarse salt flakes
1 cup **low-fat plain yogurt**
1–1½ teaspoons **horseradish**
   sauce (to taste)
1 **garlic clove**, crushed
5 cups **mixed salad greens**
1½ cups sliced **white button**
   mushrooms
1 **red onion**, thinly sliced
1 tablespoon **olive oil**
salt and **black pepper**

Rub the steaks with the crushed peppercorns and salt.

Mix together the yogurt, horseradish sauce, and garlic in a bowl and season to taste with salt and black pepper. Add the salad greens, mushrooms, and most of the red onion and toss gently.

Heat the oil in a skillet, add the steaks, and cook over high heat for 2 minutes, until browned. Turn over and cook for another 2 minutes for medium rare, 3–4 minutes for medium, or 5 minutes for well done.

Spoon the salad greens into the center of 6 serving plates. Thinly slice the steaks and arrange the pieces on top, then garnish with the remaining red onion.

For lemon beef with mustard dressing, trim the steaks and season with salt and a light grinding of black pepper. Make the salad as above, replacing the yogurt with 1 cup low-fat crème fraîche or Greek yogurt and using 2 tablespoons whole-grain mustard instead of the horseradish. Cook the steaks as above, adding the juice of ½ lemon to the skillet after removing the steaks from the heat. Turn the steaks in the lemon a couple of times, then serve as above.

lentil & goat cheese salad

Calories per serving **250**
Serves **2**
Preparation time **15 minutes**
Cooking time **20–25 minutes**

1 teaspoon **olive oil**
1 teaspoon **cumin seeds**
1 **garlic clove**, crushed
1 teaspoon peeled and grated
   fresh ginger root
¼ cup **dried green lentils**,
   well rinsed
1⅔ cups hot **chicken** or
   Vegetable Stock
   (see page 48)
1 tablespoon chopped **mint**
1 tablespoon chopped
   cilantro
squeeze of **lime juice**
3 cups **baby spinach leaves**
⅓ cup crumbled **goat cheese**
black pepper

Heat the oil in a saucepan, add the cumin seeds, garlic, and ginger, and cook, stirring, for 1 minute. Add the lentils and cook for another 1 minute.

Add the hot stock to the pan, one ladleful at a time, allowing the liquid to be absorbed before adding more, and cook until the lentils for 15–20 minutes, until tender Remove the pan from the heat and stir in the herbs and lime juice.

Divide the spinach leaves between 2 serving bowls, top with the lentils and goat cheese, and sprinkle with black pepper.

For lentil & goat cheese soup, cook the cumin seeds, garlic, and ginger in the oil as above, then add 1 (15 oz) can green lentils or 2 cups cooked dried green lentils and 2½ cups hot vegetable stock and simmer for 10 minutes. Stir in the herbs and lime juice. Blend the soup with an immersion blender until smooth, adding a little more stock, if needed, or transfer to a blender or food processor. Return to the pan and reheat gently, if necessary. Stir through 2 tablespoons low-fat plain yogurt, season to taste with salt and black pepper, and serve sprinkled with the crumbled goat cheese.

chicken burgers & tomato salsa

Calories per serving **299**
Serves **4**
Preparation time **15 minutes**,
  plus chilling
Cooking time **6–8 minutes**

1 **garlic clove**, crushed
3 **scallions**, finely sliced
1 tablespoon **pesto**
2 tablespoons chopped **mixed
  herbs**, such as parsley,
  tarragon, and thyme
12 oz **ground chicken**
2 **sun-dried tomatoes**,
  finely chopped
1 teaspoon **olive oil**

Tomato salsa
1¾ cups quartered **cherry
  tomatoes**
1 **red chile**, seeded and finely
  chopped
1 tablespoon chopped
  cilantro
grated rind and juice of **1 lime**

To serve
toasted **whole-wheat burger
  bun**
mixed salad greens

Mix together all the burger ingredients, except the oil, in a bowl. Divide the mixture into 4 and form into patties. Cover and chill for 30 minutes.

Meanwhile, combine all the salsa ingredients in a bowl.

Brush the burgers with oil and cook under a preheated hot broiler or on a barbecue for 3–4 minutes on each side until cooked through.

Serve each burger in a toasted burger bun with the tomato salsa and salad greens.

For turkey burgers with mint & yogurt sauce, make the burgers as above, replacing the ground chicken with 12 oz lean ground turkey. Instead of the salsa, make a sauce by combining ⅓ cup low-fat plain yogurt, 1 seeded and finely chopped red chile, 1 tablespoon coarsely chopped mint, and a large pinch of ground cumin in a bowl. Cook and serve the burgers as above with the mint and yogurt sauce.

ginger scallops with asparagus

Calories per serving **248**
Serves **4**
Preparation time **10 minutes**,
  plus marinating
Cooking time **8–10 minutes**

12 **scallops**
2 **scallions**, thinly sliced
finely grated zest of **1 lime**
1 tablespoon **ginger syrup**
  (from a jar of preserved
  ginger)
2 tablespoons **extra-virgin
  olive oil**, plus extra for
  drizzling
8 oz thin **asparagus spears**
juice of ½ **lime**
mixed salad greens
salt and **black pepper**
chervil sprigs, to garnish

Cut each scallop in half and place the pieces in a
nonmetallic bowl.

Mix together the scallions, lime zest, ginger syrup,
and half the oil in a separate bowl. Season to taste and
pour this dressing over the scallops. Let marinate for
15 minutes.

Meanwhile, put the asparagus in a steamer, cover,
and cook for 5–8 minutes, until tender. Toss with the
remaining oil and the lime juice. Season to taste and
keep warm.

Heat a large nonstick skillet until hot, add the scallops,
and cook for 1 minute on each side, until golden and
just cooked through. Add the marinade juices and
heat through.

Arrange the asparagus spears, salad greens, and
chervil sprigs on 4 serving plates with the scallops
and any pan juices, then serve.

For scallops with prosciutto, wash and cut the
scallops, then marinate in 2 crushed garlic cloves, the
lime zest, and all the oil, omitting the scallions and
ginger syrup. Meanwhile, remove the fat from 4 slices of
prosciutto, then cook under a preheated hot broiler for
2–3 minutes, until golden and crisp. Let cool, then break
the ham into large pieces. Cook the scallops as above
and serve with the ham and remaining ingredients. Omit
the asparagus.

crab & cilantro cakes

Calories per serving **185**
Serves **6**
Preparation time **20 minutes**
Cooking time **10 minutes**

2 (6 oz) **cans crabmeat**,
  drained
1¼ cups **cold mashed**
  potatoes
2 tablespoons chopped
  cilantro
bunch of **scallions**,
  finely sliced
grated zest and juice of
  ½ **lemon**
2 **eggs**, beaten
flour, for coating
3 cups **fresh white**
  bread crumbs
1 tablespoon **vegetable oil**
lime wedges, to serve

Mix together, the crabmeat, mashed potatoes, cilantro, scallions, and lemon zest and juice in a large bowl with half the beaten egg to bind.

Form the mixture into 12 cakes about ½ inch thick. Coat the cakes with flour, then dip into the remaining egg and then the bread crumbs.

Heat the oil in a nonstick skillet and cook the cakes for about 10 minutes, until golden, turning once or twice.

Drain the cakes on paper towels, then serve 2 cakes per person with a sweet red chili sauce or tomato salsa, if desired (remembering to count the extra calories), and with lime wedges.

For cod & dill cakes, prepare the cakes as above, using 12 oz cooked cod fillet, skinned and flaked, in place of the crabmeat and 2 tablespoons chopped dill instead of the cilantro. Add 2 tablespoons drained and chopped capers to the mix before shaping, coating, and cooking as above. Serve with a little reduced-fat sour cream.

parsley & garlic sardines

Calories per serving **180**
Serves **6**
Preparation time **10 minutes**,
  plus chilling (optional)
Cooking time **5 minutes**

12 **fresh sardines**, cleaned,
  or use fillets if preferred

Marinade
1 cup chopped **parsley**
1 teaspoon **freshly ground
  black pepper**
1 **garlic clove**, crushed
finely grated zest and juice
  of 1 **lemon**
2 tablespoons **white wine**
1 tablespoon **olive oil**

Put all the marinade ingredients into a small saucepan. Bring to a boil, then remove from the heat.

Place the sardines on a prepared barbecue, on a preheated hot ridged grill pan, or under a hot broiler. Cook for 1–2 minutes on each side, until crisp and golden.

Arrange the sardines in a single layer in a shallow serving dish. Pour the dressing over the sardines and serve hot. Alternatively, cover and chill for at least 1 hour before serving cold.

For harissa & almond sardines, combine the ingredients for the marinade in a bowl, replacing the white wine with 1½ teaspoons harissa paste. Cook the sardines as above, arrange in a shallow dish, then spoon the prepared marinade over the fish. Cover and chill for at least 1 hour, occasionally turning the sardines in the marinade. Sprinkle with 1 tablespoon toasted slivered almonds and serve as above.

lettuce wrappers with crab

Calories per serving **50**
Serves **4**
Preparation time **30 minutes**

1 fresh cooked crab
  (about 1 lb), cleaned
4 small **iceberg lettuce**
  leaves
salt and **black pepper**

Cucumber relish
¼ **cucumber**, finely diced
3 **scallions**, thinly sliced
½ large **red chile**, seeded
  and finely chopped
2 tablespoons **white wine**
  vinegar
1 teaspoon **light soy sauce**
1 teaspoon **granulated sugar**
4 teaspoons finely chopped
  mint or **cilantro**

Make the relish by mixing all the ingredients in a bowl with a little salt and black pepper.

Twist and remove the 2 large claws and spiderlike legs from the crab and set aside. With the crab upside down, pull away the ball-like, spongy lungs. Check that the small sac and any green matter have been removed, then scoop the brown meat and skin from under the shell onto a plate. Break up the crabmeat with a spoon.

Put the crab claws into a plastic bag and hit once or twice with a rolling pin to break the shells. Then, working on one claw at a time, peel away the shell, removing the white flesh with a small knife and a skewer. Add to the brown crabmeat.

When ready to serve, spoon the crab into the lettuce leaves and top with spoonfuls of the cucumber relish. Roll up and eat with your fingers.

For lettuce wrappers with spicy shrimp, make the relish as above. Toss 11½ oz peeled jumbo shrimp in 1½ teaspoons Thai red curry paste in a bowl until well coated. Cover and chill for 30 minutes. Heat 2 teaspoons peanut oil in a nonstick skillet, add the shrimp, and stir-fry for 3–4 minutes, until they turn pink and are cooked through. Toss the shrimp into the relish and serve spooned into the lettuce leaves.

jumbo shrimp with pancetta

Calories per serving **187**
Serves **4**
Preparation time **5 minutes**
Cooking time **7–8 minutes**

1 teaspoon **olive oil**
1 teaspoon **unsalted butter**
2 oz **pancetta** or **smoked bacon**, excess fat removed, finely chopped
1 lb **jumbo shrimp,** peeled but tails left intact
grated zest and juice of 1 **lemon**
large bunch of **watercress**

Heat the oil and butter in a skillet, add the pancetta or smoked bacon, and cook for 3–4 minutes, until crisp.

Add the shrimp and cook for 1 minute on each side or until they turn pink. Sprinkle with the lemon zest and juice and cook for another 1 minute, then add the watercress and combine well. Divide among 4 plates and serve immediately.

For jumbo shrimp & chorizo with arugula, omit the olive oil, butter, and pancetta. Finely slice 2 oz chorizo and dry-fry in a large nonstick skillet over low heat until crispy and some of its juices have been released. Increase the heat to high, toss in the shrimp, and continue as above, replacing the watercress with 3½ cups arugula.

chile & cilantro fish package

Calories per serving **127**
Serves **1**
Preparation time **15 minutes**,
  plus marinating and chilling
Cooking time **15 minutes**

4 oz **cod**, **halibut**, or
  haddock fillet
2 teaspoons **fresh lemon juice**
1 tablespoon **cilantro leaves**
1 **garlic clove**
1 **green chile**, seeded
  and chopped
¼ teaspoon **sugar**
2 teaspoons **low-fat**
  plain yogurt

To garnish
cilantro sprigs
sliced **green chiles**

Place the fish in a nonmetallic dish and sprinkle with the lemon juice. Cover and let marinate in the refrigerator for 15–20 minutes.

Put the cilantro, garlic, and chile in a food processor or blender and process until the mixture forms a paste. Add the sugar and yogurt and briefly process to blend.

Lay the fish on a sheet of aluminum foil. Coat the fish on both sides with the paste. Gather up the foil loosely and turn over at the top to seal. Chill for at least 1 hour.

Place the package on a baking sheet and bake in a preheated oven, at 400°F, for about 15 minutes, until the fish is just cooked through.

Garnish with cilantro sprigs and sliced green chiles and serve immediately.

For scallion & ginger fish package, place the fish fillet on a sheet of aluminum foil. Omit the above marinade. Combine 1 teaspoon peeled and chopped fresh ginger root and 2 thinly sliced scallions with a pinch of granulated sugar and the juice and grated zest of ½ lime. Rub the mixture all over the fish, then seal and marinate the package as above for 30 minutes. Bake as above.

crab & noodle asian wraps

Calories per serving **199**
Serves **4**
Preparation time **15 minutes**,
    plus standing
Cooking time **5 minutes**

7 oz **rice noodles**
1 bunch of **scallions**,
    finely sliced
¾ inch piece of **fresh ginger
    root**, peeled and grated
1 **garlic clove**, finely sliced
1 **red chile**, finely chopped
2 tablespoons chopped
    cilantro
1 tablespoon chopped **mint**
¼ **cucumber**, cut into fine
    matchsticks
2 (6 oz) cans **crabmeat**,
    drained, or 10 oz **fresh
    white crabmeat**
1 tablespoon **sesame oil**
1 tablespoon **sweet chili
    sauce**
1 teaspoon **Thai fish sauce**
16 **Chinese pancakes** or
    **Vietnamese rice-paper
    wrappers**

Cook the noodles according to the package directions. Drain, then refresh under cold running water.

Mix together all the other ingredients, except the pancakes or rice-paper wrappers, in a large bowl. Add the noodles and toss to mix. Cover and let stand for 10 minutes to allow the flavors to develop, then transfer to a serving dish.

To serve, top the pancakes or rice papers with some of the crab-and-noodle mixture and roll up to eat, allowing 4 wraps per person.

For shrimp & peanut wraps, make the mixture as above, replacing the crab with 7 oz small cooked, peeled shrimp and adding 2 tablespoons chopped peanuts. Stir in the juice of 1 lime and wrap as above.

red pepper & feta rolls with olives

Calories per serving **146**
Serves **4**
Preparation time **15 minutes**,
plus cooling
Cooking time **7–8 minutes**

2 **red bell peppers**, cored,
seeded, and quartered
lengthwise
3½ oz **feta cheese**, thinly
sliced or crumbled
16 **basil leaves**
16 **black ripe olives**, pitted
and halved
2 tablespoons **pine nuts**,
toasted
1 tablespoon **pesto**
1 tablespoon **fat-free
French dressing**

Place the bell peppers skin side up on a baking sheet under a preheated hot broiler and cook for 7–8 minutes, until the skins are blackened. Remove the bell peppers and place them in a plastic bag. Fold over the top to seal and let cool for 20 minutes, then remove the skins.

Lay the skinned bell pepper quarters on a board and layer up the feta, basil, olives, and pine nuts on each one.

Carefully roll up the bell peppers and secure each one with a toothpick. Place 2 pepper rolls on each of 4 serving plates.

Whisk together the pesto and French dressing in a small bowl and drizzle it over the pepper rolls. Serve with arugula, if desired (remembering to count the extra calories).

For red pepper, ricotta & sun-dried tomato rolls, broil and skin the bell peppers as above. Mix 5 chopped sun-dried tomatoes into 3½ oz ricotta cheese, also stirring in the basil and pine nuts. Omit the feta and black ripe olives. Season with salt and black pepper and use to top the bell pepper quarters. Roll up and serve as above.

caponata ratatouille

Calories per serving **90**
Serves **6**
Preparation time **20 minutes**
Cooking time **40 minutes**

1 tablespoon **olive oil**
1 large **eggplant**, cut into
 ½ inch chunks
1 large **onion**, cut into
 ½ inch chunks
3 **celery sticks**, coarsely
 chopped
a little **wine** (optional)
2 large **beefsteak tomatoes**,
 skinned (see page 162)
 and seeded
1 teaspoon chopped **thyme**
¼–½ teaspoon **cayenne**
 pepper
2 tablespoons **capers**, drained
handful of **pitted green olives**
¼ cup **white wine vinegar**
1 tablespoon **sugar**
1–2 tablespoons
 unsweetened cocoa
 powder (optional)
black pepper

To garnish
toasted, chopped **almonds**
chopped **parsley**

Heat the oil in a nonstick skillet until hot, add the eggplant, and sauté for about 15 minutes, until soft. Add a little boiling water to prevent it from sticking, if necessary.

Meanwhile, put the onion and celery into a saucepan with a little wine or water. Cook for 5 minutes, until tender but still firm.

Add the tomatoes, thyme, cayenne pepper and eggplant to the onion and celery. Cook for 15 minutes, stirring occasionally. Add the capers, olives, wine vinegar, sugar and cocoa powder, if using, and cook for 2–3 minutes.

Season with black pepper and sprinkle with the almonds and parsley. Divide among 6 bowls and serve immediately.

For red pepper & zucchini caponata, broil and skin 2 red and 2 yellow bell peppers (see page 80). Cook the onion and celery as above, then continue as above, adding the skinned bell peppers and 3 thickly sliced zucchini instead of the eggplants, and omitting the thyme and cocoa powder.

zucchini & mint frittatas

Calories per serving **200**
Serves **6**
Preparation time **10 minutes**
Cooking time **about**
  30 minutes

1 tablespoon **olive oil**
1 **onion**, finely chopped
2 **zucchini**, halved lengthwise
  and thinly sliced
6 **eggs**
1¼ cups **skim milk**
3 tablespoons grated
  Parmesan cheese
2 tablespoons chopped **mint**,
  plus extra leaves to garnish
  (optional)
salt and **black pepper**

Tomato sauce
1 tablespoon **olive oil**
1 **onion**, finely chopped
1–2 **garlic cloves**, crushed
  (optional)
8 **plum tomatoes**, chopped

Lightly oil a 12-section muffin pan.

Make the sauce. Heat the oil in a saucepan, add the onion, and sauté for 5 minutes, stirring occasionally, until softened and just beginning to brown. Add the garlic, if using, and the tomatoes and season with salt and black pepper. Stir and simmer for 5 minutes, until the tomatoes are soft. Puree in a blender or food processor until smooth, then pass through a strainer into a bowl and keep warm.

Heat the oil in a skillet, add the onion, and sauté until softened and just beginning to brown. Add the zucchini, stir to combine, and cook for 3–4 minutes, until softened but not browned.

Beat together the eggs, milk, Parmesan, and mint in a bowl, then stir in the zucchini. Season well and divide the mixture between the 12 sections of the prepared pan. Bake in a preheated oven, at 375°F, for about 15 minutes, until lightly browned, well risen, and the egg mixture has set.

Let the frittatas stand in the pan for 1–2 minutes, then loosen the edges with a knife. Turn out and arrange on 6 plates with the warm tomato sauce. Garnish with extra mint leaves, if desired.

For garlicky arugula frittatas, make the tomato sauce to serve as above. For the frittatas, omit the zucchini. Soften the onions as above, then add 2 crushed garlic cloves, stir for 1 minute, and remove from the heat. Beat together the eggs, milk, and Parmesan as above, replacing the mint with 3 cups coarsely chopped arugula. Add the cooked onions and bake as above.

goat cheese & herb souffles

Calories per souffle **277**
Serves **4**
Preparation time **10 minutes**
Cooking time **13–15 minutes**

2 tablespoons
  polyunsaturated margarine
⅓ cup **all-purpose flour**
1¼ cups **skim milk**
4 **eggs**, separated
⅔ cup crumbled **goat cheese**
1 tablespoon chopped **mixed
  herbs**, such as parsley,
  chives, and thyme
1 tablespoon grated
  Parmesan cheese
3 cups **arugula leaves**
2 tablespoons **fat-free salad
  dressing**
salt and **black pepper**

Melt the margarine in a medium saucepan, add the flour, and cook, stirring, for 1 minute. Gradually add the milk, whisking all the time, and cook for 2 minutes, until the roux has thickened.

Remove the pan from the heat. Beat in the egg yolks, one at a time, then stir in the goat cheese. Season well with salt and black pepper.

Whisk the egg whites in a large bowl until they form firm peaks, then gradually fold them into the cheese mixture with the herbs. Transfer to 4 lightly oiled ramekins, sprinkle with the Parmesan, then bake in a preheated oven, at 375°F, for 10–12 minutes, until risen and golden.

Toss together the arugula and dressing in a bowl and serve with the souffles.

For Gruyère & mustard souffle, cook the flour in the margarine as above, stirring in 2 teaspoons English mustard powder. Continue as above, replacing the goat cheese with ¾ cup shredded Gruyère cheese and omitting the Parmesan.

chile & melon sorbet with ham

Calories per serving **125**
Serves **6**
Preparation time **35 minutes**,
  plus freezing

1 ½ **cantaloupes**, quartered
  and seeded
12 slices of **Serrano ham** or
  prosciutto, fat removed

Sorbet
1 **cantaloupe**, halved, peeled,
  and seeded
2 tablespoons chopped **mint**
½–1 large **red chile**, seeded
  and finely chopped (to taste),
  plus strips of chile to garnish
1 **egg white**

Make the sorbet. Scoop the melon flesh into a food processor or blender and blend until smooth. Stir in the mint and add chile to taste.

Transfer the mixture to an ice cream maker and churn until thick. Alternatively, pour the mixture into a plastic container and freeze for 4 hours, beating once or twice to break up the ice crystals.

Mix in the egg white and continue churning until the sorbet is thick enough to scoop. If you are not serving it immediately, transfer the sorbet to a plastic container and store in the freezer. Otherwise, freeze for a minimum of 2 hours until firm.

Arrange the melon quarters and ham on 6 serving plates. Use warm spoons to scoop out the sorbet and put 2 spoonfuls of sorbet on top of each melon quarter. Garnish with strips of chile and serve immediately.

For honeyed peaches, to serve with the ham instead of the sorbet and melon quarters, make a dressing using 1 tablespoon extra virgin olive oil, 2 tablespoons chopped mint, ½ seeded and finely chopped red chile, and 1 teaspoon honey. Cut 5 peaches into wedges and stir into the dressing. Let marinate for 30 minutes, then serve with the ham slices.

red pepper rouille & vegetables

Calories per serving **154**
Serves **6**
Preparation time **30 minutes**,
    plus marinating and cooling
Cooking time **30–35 minutes**

¼ cup **olive oil**
2–3 **garlic cloves**, finely
    chopped
3 large pinches of **saffron
    threads**
3 mixed **red** and **orange bell
    peppers**, cored, seeded, and
    each cut into 6 strips
3 small **zucchini**
2 **onions**, cut into wedges
salt and **black pepper**

Rouille
4 **plum tomatoes**
1 **red bell pepper**, cored,
    seeded, and quartered
1 **garlic clove**, finely chopped
large pinch of **ground
    pimentón** (smoked paprika)
1 tablespoon **olive oil**

Put the oil for the vegetables in a large plastic bag with the garlic, saffron, and salt and black pepper. Add the vegetables, grip the top edge of the bag to seal, and toss together. Let marinate for at least 30 minutes.

Make the rouille. Put the tomatoes and red bell pepper into a roasting pan. Sprinkle with the garlic, pimentón, and salt and black pepper, then drizzle with the oil. Roast in a preheated oven, at 425°F, for 15 minutes.

Let cool, then peel the skins from the tomatoes and bell pepper. Puree the flesh in a blender or food processor with any juices from the roasting pan until smooth. Spoon into a serving bowl and set aside.

Transfer the saffron vegetables into a large roasting pan and cook in a preheated oven, at 425°F, for 15–20 minutes, turning once until browned. Spoon the vegetables into 6 bowls and serve with spoonfuls of the rouille, reheated if necessary.

For potato puffs, to serve with the rouille instead of the saffron vegetables, cut 2 lb new potatoes in half and lay them, cut side up, in a single layer in an ovenproof dish. Sprinkle with sea salt and black pepper and roast (without any oil) in a preheated oven, at 425°F, for 30–35 minutes, until cooked through and puffed up. Serve with the rouille.

vietnamese-style noodle salad

Calories per serving **271**
Serves **4**
Preparation time **20 minutes**
Cooking time **4 minutes**

7 oz **fine rice noodles**
½ **cucumber**, seeded and cut
   into matchsticks
1 **carrot**, cut into matchsticks
1½ cups **bean sprouts**
2 cups **snow peas**,
   cut into thin strips
2 tablespoons chopped
   cilantro
2 tablespoons chopped **mint**
1 **red chile**, seeded and
   finely sliced
2 tablespoons chopped
   unsalted peanuts,
   to garnish

Dressing
1 tablespoon **sunflower** or
   peanut oil
½ teaspoon **granulated sugar**
1 tablespoon **Thai fish sauce**
2 tablespoons **lime juice**

Bring a large saucepan of water to a boil, then turn off
the heat and add the rice noodles. Cover and let cook
for 4 minutes, or according to the package directions,
until just tender. Drain the noodles and cool immediately
in a bowl of ice-cold water.

Meanwhile, make the dressing by placing the ingredients
in a screw-top jar, adding the lid and shaking until the
sugar has dissolved.

Drain the noodles and return to the bowl. Pour half
of the dressing over the noodles, then top with the
vegetables, herbs, and chile. Toss until well combined.

Pile the noodle salad onto 4 serving plates and drizzle
with the remaining dressing. Serve sprinkled with the
chopped peanuts.

green bean & asparagus salad

Calories per serving **285**
Serves **6**
Preparation time **10 minutes**
Cooking time **8 minutes**

2½ cups trimmed
   green beans
13 oz **asparagus**, trimmed
6 **eggs**
3½ cups **arugula leaves**
¾ cup **pitted black**
   ripe olives
3 oz **Parmesan cheese**, cut
   into shavings
salt and **black pepper**

Dressing
⅓ cup **olive oil**
1 tablespoon **black olive**
   pesto or **tapenade**
1 tablespoon **balsamic**
   vinegar

Put the green beans in the top of a steamer, cover, and cook for 3 minutes. Add the asparagus and cook for another 5 minutes, until the vegetables are just tender.

Meanwhile, put the eggs into a small saucepan, cover with cold water, and bring to a boil. Simmer for 6 minutes, until still soft in the center.

Make the dressing by mixing together the oil, pesto, and vinegar in a small bowl with a little salt and black pepper.

Arrange the arugula in the center of 6 serving plates. Drain and rinse the eggs with cold water. Drain again, gently peel away the shells, and halve each egg. Place 2 halves on each mound of arugula. Arrange the beans and asparagus around the edge, then drizzle with the dressing. Add the olives and top with the Parmesan shavings. Serve immediately.

For baby broccoli & olive salad, omit the beans and asparagus and steam 1 lb baby broccoli as above for 5 minutes. Cook the eggs as above, shell, and quarter. Arrange the arugula on 6 plates, then sprinkle with the eggs and baby broccoli. Continue with the dressing, olives and Parmesan as above.

potato & onion tortilla

Calories per serving **296**
Serves **6**
Preparation time **10 minutes**
Cooking time **30 minutes**

6 **baking potatoes**, peeled
 and sliced thinly
¼ cup **olive oil**
2 large **onions**, thinly sliced
6 **eggs**, beaten
salt and **black pepper**

Toss the potatoes in a bowl with a little seasoning. Heat the oil in a medium, heavy skillet, add the potatoes, and sauté gently for 10 minutes, turning frequently, until softened but not browned.

Add the onions and sauté gently for another 5 minutes without browning. Spread the potatoes and onions in an even layer in the pan, then reduce the heat as low as possible.

Pour the eggs over the potatoes, cover, and cook gently for about 15 minutes, until the eggs have set. (If the center of the omelet is too wet, put the pan under a preheated medium broiler to finish cooking.) Transfer the tortilla onto a plate, cut into 6 wedges, and serve warm or cold with a arugula, herb, and tomato salad, if desired (remembering to count the extra calories).

For bell pepper & artichoke tortilla, drain 3½ oz of marinated artichokes in olive oil, reserving the oil. Heat 1 tablespoon of the oil in a skillet and cook 2 red and 1 yellow cored, seeded, and sliced bell peppers for 5–6 minutes, until starting to soften. Coarsely chop the artichokes and add to the pan with 1 small chopped onion and 1 tablespoon chopped mint. Spread into an even layer and reduce the heat as low as possible, then pour the eggs over the top and cook as above.

mushroom crepes

Calories per serving **112**
Serves **4**
Preparation time **20 minutes**
Cooking time **30 minutes**

⅓ cup **all-purpose flour**
⅔ cup **skim milk**
1 medium **egg**, beaten
1 teaspoon **olive oil**
salt and **black pepper**
flat leaf parsley sprigs,
　to garnish

Filling
5 cups chopped **cremini
　mushrooms**
bunch of **scallions**,
　finely chopped
1 **garlic clove**, chopped
1 (14½ oz) can **diced
　tomatoes**, drained
2 tablespoons chopped
　oregano

Put the flour, milk, egg, and salt and black pepper in a blender or food processor and blend until smooth, or whisk with a fork in a bowl.

Heat a few drops of the oil in a nonstick skillet. Pour in a ladleful of the batter and cook for 1 minute. Carefully flip the crepe over, and cook the other side. Slide the crepe out of the pan onto wax paper. Make 3 more crepes in the same way, adding a few more drops of oil to the pan between each one, and stack the crepes between sheets of wax paper.

Meanwhile, make the filling. Put all the ingredients in a saucepan and cook for 5 minutes, stirring occasionally.

Divide the filling among the crepes, reserving a little of the mixture to serve, then roll them up.

Transfer to an ovenproof dish and bake in a preheated oven, at 350°F, for 20 minutes. Serve with the reheated reserved mushroom mixture, garnished with parsley.

For ratatouille-filled crepes, put 2 chopped zucchini, 1 cored, seeded, and chopped red bell pepper, 1 chopped red onion, 1 (14½ oz) can diced tomatoes, and a few basil leaves in a large saucepan and simmer for 6–8 minutes, stirring occasionally. Make the crepes as above, then fill with the zucchini mixture and bake as above.

leek & tomato phyllo tarts

Calories per serving **135**
Serves **4**
Preparation time **20 minutes**,
   plus soaking
Cooking time **30 minutes**

8 sun-dried tomatoes
2 **leeks**, trimmed and
   thinly sliced
1¼ cups **white wine**
2 tablespoons **skim milk**
1 medium **egg**, separated
¼ cup **low-fat cream cheese**
12 pieces of **phyllo pastry**,
   each about 6 inches square
salt and **black pepper**

Put the sun-dried tomatoes in a small heatproof bowl and pour over enough boiling water to cover. Let soak for 20 minutes.

Meanwhile, put the leeks and wine in a saucepan and bring to a boil, then reduce the heat and simmer until the liquid has evaporated. Remove the pan from the heat and stir in the milk, egg yolk, and cheese. Season with salt and black pepper.

Beat the egg white lightly in a small bowl. Brush a phyllo pastry square with a little of the egg white and use it to line the bottom and sides of a 4 inch tart pan. Brush 2 more phyllo squares and lay these on top, each at a slight angle to the first, allowing the edges to overlap the rim. Repeat with the remaining squares to line 3 more tart pans.

Place a spoonful of the cooked leek mixture in each pastry shell. Lay 2 of the drained, rehydrated tomatoes on top of each tart and cover with the remaining leek mixture. Season again and bake in a preheated oven, at 400°F, for 20 minutes, covering the tarts with pieces of aluminum foil after 10 minutes. Serve hot, with cherry tomatoes and sliced red onion, if desired (remembering to count the extra calories).

red pepper & scallion dip

Calories per serving
  (dip only) **60**
Serves **4**
Preparation time **10 minutes**
Cooking time **30–40 minutes**

1 large **red bell pepper**,
  cored, seeded, and
  quartered
2 **garlic cloves**, unpeeled
1 cup **low-fat plain yogurt**
2 **scallions**, finely chopped,
  plus extra to garnish
black pepper
selection of **raw vegetables**,
  such as carrots, cucumber,
  bel peppers, fennel,
  tomatoes, baby corn, snow
  peas, celery, and zucchini,
  cut into batons, to serve

Slightly flatten the bell pepper quarters and place on a baking sheet. Wrap the garlic in aluminum foil and place on the sheet. Roast in a preheated oven, at 425°F, for 30–40 minutes, until the bell pepper is slightly charred and the garlic is soft.

When cool enough to handle, remove the skin from the bell pepper and discard. Transfer the flesh to a bowl.

Squeeze the roasted garlic flesh from the cloves into the bowl.

Using a fork, coarsely mash the bell pepper and garlic together. Stir in the yogurt and scallions.

Garnish with extra chopped scallion, season to taste with black pepper, and serve with the vegetable batons.

For eggplant & yogurt dip, roast a whole eggplant in a preheated oven, at 425°F, with the garlic for 30–40 minutes, omitting the red bell pepper. If the eggplant is still not tender after the cooking time, carefully turn it over and bake for 10–15 minutes, until soft. Cut the eggplant in half and scoop the flesh out onto a cutting board. Coarsely chop with a handful of basil leaves and season with salt and black pepper. Stir into the yogurt and scallions, and add the roasted garlic. Serve with the vegetable batons.

main meals

butternut squash & ricotta frittata

Calories per serving **248**
Serves **6**
Preparation time **10 minutes**
Cooking time **25–30 minutes**

1 tablespoon **extra virgin canola oil**
1 **red onion**, thinly sliced
1 **butternut squash**, peeled, seeded, and diced
8 **eggs**
2 tablespoons chopped **sage**
1 tablespoon chopped **thyme**
½ cup **ricotta cheese**
salt and **black pepper**

Heat the oil in a large, deep skillet with an ovenproof handle over medium-low heat, add the onion and butternut squash, then cover loosely and cook gently, stirring frequently, for 18–20 minutes, until softened and golden.

Beat together the eggs, herbs, and ricotta lightly in a small bowl, then season well with salt and bell pepper and pour the eggs over the squash mixture.

Cook for 2–3 minutes, until the eggs are almost set, stirring occasionally to prevent the bottom from burning.

Slide the pan under a preheated broiler, keeping the handle away from the heat, and cook for 3–4 minutes, until the eggs are set and the frittata is golden. Slice into 6 wedges and serve hot.

For poached egg-topped butternut salad, toss the diced butternut squash and thickly sliced red onion in the canola oil in a roasting pan and roast in a preheated oven, at 400°F, for 20 minutes. Remove from the oven and let cool while you poach the eggs. Bring a saucepan of water to a boil, swirl the water with a spoon, and crack in an egg, allowing the white to wrap around the yolk. Simmer for 3 minutes, then remove and keep warm. Repeat with 5 more eggs. Toss the warm roasted squash and onion with 4 cups baby spinach leaves and divide among 6 serving plates. Top each salad with a poached egg, then spoon a little ricotta cheese over each, sprinkle with the herbs, and serve.

lamb cutlets with herbed crust

Calories per serving **280**
Serves **4**
Preparation time **10 minutes**
Cooking time **12–14 minutes**

12 **lean lamb cutlet**
   (about 1½ oz each)
2 tablespoons **pesto**
3 tablespoons **multigrain**
   bread crumbs
1 tablespoon chopped
   walnuts, toasted
1 teaspoon **vegetable oil**
2 **garlic cloves**, crushed
1¼ lb **collard greens**, finely
   shredded and blanched

Heat a nonstick skillet until hot, add the cutlets, and cook for 1 minute on each side, then transfer to a baking sheet.

Mix together the pesto, bread crumbs, and walnuts in a bowl, then use to top one side of the cutlets, pressing down lightly. Place in a preheated oven, at 400°F, for 10–12 minutes.

Meanwhile, heat the oil in a skillet or wok, add the garlic, and stir-fry for 1 minute, then add the greens and stir-fry for another 3–4 minutes, until tender.

Serve the lamb and greens with some baby carrots, if desired (remembering to count the extra calories).

For lamb cutlets with herbed caper dressing, make a dressing by combining 1 tablespoon each of chopped flat leaf parsley, mint, and basil in a small bowl. Stir in 1 crushed garlic clove, 1 tablespoon drained and chopped capers, and 2 tablespoons extra-virgin olive oil. Cook the cutlets in a hot skillet for 2–3 minutes on each side, depending on whether you like your lamb medium or well done, omit the bread crumb topping, and serve with the vegetables as above and a generous drizzle of the dressing.

beef skewers with dipping sauce

Calories per serving **140**
Serves **4**
Preparation time **10 minutes**,
plus marinating
Cooking time **2–3 minutes**

1 tablespoon **sweet chili
sauce**
½ teaspoon **cumin seeds,**
toasted
½ teaspoon **ground coriander**
1 teaspoon **olive oil**
11½ oz **lean top sirloin
steak**, cut into strips

Dipping sauce
1 tablespoon **sweet chili
sauce**
1 teaspoon **Thai fish sauce**
1 teaspoon **white wine
vinegar**

To serve
2 tablespoons chopped
cilantro
1 tablespoon **unsalted
peanuts**, coarsely chopped

Mix together the sweet chili sauce, cumin seeds, ground coriander, and oil in a nonmetallic bowl. Add the meat and stir well to coat, then cover and let marinate in a cool place for 30 minutes.

Thread the meat onto 4 bamboo skewers that have been soaked in water for at least 20 minutes. Cook on a hot ridged grill pan or under a preheated hot broiler for 2–3 minutes, until cooked through.

Meanwhile, mix together the sauce ingredients in a small serving bowl. Serve the skewers with the sauce, sprinkled with the cilantro and peanuts.

For Thai-style salad, to serve with the skewers, combine 1 grated carrot, ¼ thinly sliced cucumber, and 10 quartered cherry tomatoes in a bowl. Make the dipping sauce as above, adding 1 teaspoon peanut oil. Toss it into the salad ingredients with the cilantro and peanuts used as garnish above, and serve the skewers with the salad and lime wedges.

chicken & spinach curry

Calories per serving **205**
Serves **4**
Preparation time **15 minutes**
Cooking time **25 minutes**

1 tablespoon **vegetable oil**
4 **skinless, boneless chicken breasts** (about 4 oz each),
   halved lengthwise
1 **onion**, sliced
2 **garlic cloves**, chopped
1 **green chile**, chopped
4 **cardamom pods**, lightly
   crushed
1 teaspoon **cumin seeds**
1 teaspoon **dried red pepper flakes**
1 teaspoon **ground ginger**
1 teaspoon **ground turmeric**
8 cups **baby spinach leaves**
3 **tomatoes**, chopped
⅔ cup **low-fat Greek yogurt**
2 tablespoons chopped
   cilantro, plus extra sprigs
   to garnish

Heat the oil in a large skillet or wok, add the chicken, onion, garlic, and chile, and sauté for 4–5 minutes, until the chicken begins to brown and the onion softens. Add the cardamoms, cumin seeds, dried red pepper flakes, ginger, and turmeric and cook for another 1 minute.

Add the spinach, cover, and cook gently until the spinach wilts, then stir in the tomatoes, replace the lid, and simmer for 15 minutes or until the chicken is cooked through, removing the lid for the last 5 minutes of cooking.

Stir the yogurt and chopped cilantro into the curry, then sprinkle with cilantro sprigs to garnish. Serve with boiled rice, if desired (remembering to count the extra calories).

For curried chicken kebabs & spinach salad,
cut the chicken into strips and put in a nonmetallic bowl with 1 chopped onion and 4 quartered tomatoes, then toss with the garlic, chile, and spices. Thread onto 8 metal skewers, then cook under a preheated broiler for 4–5 minutes on each side or until the chicken is cooked through. Meanwhile, make a raita by mixing together ⅔ cup low-fat plain yogurt, ½ cucumber, grated, and 2 tablespoons chopped mint in a bowl. Serve 2 kebabs per person on a bed of baby spinach leaves with the raita.

thai-style monkfish kebabs

Calories per serving **192**
Serves **4**
Preparation time **15 minutes**,
  plus marinating
Cooking time **10 minutes**

1–1½ lb **monkfish tails**,
  skinned and cut into
  large cubes
1 **onion**, quartered and
  layers separated
8 **mushrooms**
1 **zucchini**, cut into 8 pieces
vegetable oil, for brushing
lime wedges, to serve

Marinade
grated zest and juice of 2 **limes**
1 **garlic clove**, finely chopped
2 tablespoons peeled
  and finely sliced **fresh**
  ginger root
2 **chiles**, red or green or
  1 of each, seeded and finely
  chopped
2 **lemon grass stalks**,
  finely chopped
handful of chopped **cilantro**
1 glass **red wine**
2 tablespoons **sesame oil**
black pepper

Combine the ingredients for the marinade in a large nonmetallic bowl. Add the fish to the marinade with the onion, mushrooms, and zucchini and mix until well coated. Cover and let marinate in the refrigerator for 1 hour.

Brush the rack of a broiler pan lightly with oil to prevent the kebabs from sticking. Thread 4 metal skewers alternately with the chunks of fish, mushrooms, zucchini, and onion. Brush with a little oil and cook under a preheated hot broiler for about 10 minutes, turning at intervals, until cooked through. Serve with lime wedges for squeezing over the kebabs.

For Mediterranean monkfish kebabs, replace the above marinade with one using the grated zest and juice of 1 lemon, 2 chopped garlic cloves, 2 tablespoons olive oil, and 1 tablespoon each of chopped thyme and rosemary. Use to marinate the monkfish and vegetables for 30 minutes, then thread onto 4 metal skewers and cook as above.

baked squash & goat cheese

Calories per serving **230**
Serves **4**
Preparation time **20 minutes**
Cooking time **25–30 minutes**

5 **raw beets**, peeled and diced
1 large **acorn squash**,
    ½ **butternut squash**, or
    1¼ lb of **pumpkin**, peeled,
    seeded, and cut into small
    wedges or dice slightly than
    the beet dice
1 **red onion**, cut into wedges
2 tablespoons **olive oil**
2 teaspoons **fennel seeds**
2 small **goat cheeses**
    (3½ oz each)
salt and **black pepper**
chopped **rosemary**, to garnish

Put the vegetables into a roasting pan, drizzle with the oil, and sprinkle with the fennel seeds and salt and black pepper. Roast in a preheated oven, at 400°F, for 20–25 minutes, turning once, until well browned and tender.

Cut the goat cheeses into thirds and nestle among the roasted vegetables. Sprinkle the cheeses with a little salt and black pepper and drizzle with some of the pan juices.

Return the dish to the oven and cook for about 5 minutes, until the cheese is just beginning to melt. Sprinkle with rosemary and serve immediately.

For penne with beet & squash, roast the vegetables as above for 20–25 minutes, omitting the fennel seeds. Cook 6 oz penne pasta in a saucepan of salted boiling water, then drain, reserving one ladleful of the cooking water. Return the pasta to the pan and add the roasted vegetables, a handful of torn basil leaves, and the reserved cooking water. Omit the goat cheese and rosemary. Place over high heat, stirring, for 30 seconds and serve.

russian meatballs

Calories per serving **154**
Serves **4**
Preparation time **15 minutes**,
   plus chilling
Cooking time **about 1 hour**

12 oz **ground round** or
   ground sirloin beef
1 **onion**, coarsely chopped
1 tablespoon **tomato paste**
1 teaspoon **dried mixed
   herbs**
salt and **black pepper**
chopped **parsley** and **parsley
   sprigs**, to garnish

Tomato sauce
1 **red onion**, finely chopped
1 (14½ oz) can **diced
   tomatoes**
pinch of **paprika**, plus extra
   to garnish
1 teaspoon **dried mixed
   herbs**

Put the ground beef, onion, tomato paste, and dried mixed herbs in a food processor, season well with salt and black pepper, and blend until smooth. Shape the mixture into 12 balls, cover, and chill for 30 minutes.

Meanwhile, put the tomato sauce ingredients in a saucepan and cook, uncovered, over low heat for 15–20 minutes, stirring occasionally.

Season the sauce with salt and black pepper and transfer to an ovenproof dish. Arrange the meatballs on top and place in a preheated oven, at 350°F, for 45 minutes. Sprinkle the meatballs with chopped parsley and paprika, garnish with parsley sprigs, and serve with mashed potatoes, if desired (remembering to count the extra calories).

For spicy burgers with fresh tomato salsa, mix together the ground beef, finely diced onion, tomato paste, and mixed dried herbs with 1 finely diced red chile and 1 beaten egg in a bowl. Divide the mixture into 4 and shape each into a patty. Cover and chill for 30 minutes. Meanwhile, make a tomato salsa by mixing together 1 finely chopped red onion, 10 diced cherry tomatoes, 2 tablespoons chopped cilantro, and a drizzle of balsamic vinegar in a bowl. Heat a ridged grill pan until hot, add the patties, and cook for 4–5 minutes on each side until cooked through. Serve topped with a spoonful of the tomato salsa.

herbed baked chicken

Calories per serving **275**
Serves **4**
Preparation time **10 minutes**
Cooking time **35–45 minutes**

1 lb **new potatoes**
4 **skinless chicken breasts**
  (about 4 oz each)
⅓ cup **mixed herbs**, such
  as parsley, chives, chervil,
  and mint
1 **garlic clove**, crushed
⅓ cup **low-fat crème fraîche**
  or **sour cream**
8 **baby leeks**
2 **endive heads**, halved
  lengthwise
⅔ cup **chicken stock**
black pepper

Cook the potatoes in a saucepan of boiling water for 12–15 minutes, until tender. Drain, then cut into bite-size pieces.

Make a slit lengthwise down the side of each chicken breast to form a pocket, making sure that you do not cut all the way through. Mix together the herbs, garlic and crème fraîche or sour cream, season well with black pepper, then spoon a little into each chicken pocket.

Put the leeks, endive, and potatoes in an ovenproof dish. Pour the stock over the vegetables, then lay the chicken breasts on top. Spoon the remaining crème fraîche mixture over the top, then bake in a preheated oven, at 400°F, for 25–30 minutes, until the chicken is cooked through and the vegetables are tender.

For baked chicken with fennel & potatoes, cut the potatoes in half and place them in a large ovenproof dish with 1 large fennel bulb, trimmed and cut into quarters. Omit the leeks and endive. Pour in the stock and bake in a preheated oven, at 400°F, for 20 minutes. Lay the chicken breasts over the vegetables. Combine 1 tablespoon chopped parsley with 1 tablespoon Dijon mustard and the crème fraîche or sour cream, omitting the garlic, and spoon the mixture over the chicken. Return to the oven and bake for 25–30 minutes, until cooked through.

flounder & mustard sauce

Calories per serving **182**
Serves **4**
Preparation time **10 minutes**
Cooking time **10 minutes**

1 teaspoon **olive oil**
1 small **onion**, finely chopped
1 **garlic clove**, crushed
4 **flounder** or **sole fillets**
  (about 5 oz each)
½ cup **dry white wine**
2 tablespoons **whole-grain
  mustard**
1 cup **low-fat crème fraîche**
  or **Greek yogurt**
2 tablespoons chopped
  mixed herbs

To serve
10 oz **baby new potatoes,**
  steamed
3 cups **green beans,** steamed

Heat the oil in a large skillet, add the onion and garlic, and sauté for 3 minutes, until softened.

Add the fish fillets and cook for 1 minute on each side, then add the wine and simmer to reduce by half.

Stir through the remaining ingredients and bring to a boil, then reduce the heat and simmer for 3–4 minutes, until the sauce has thickened slightly and the fish is tender. Serve with steamed baby new potatoes and green beans.

For salmon with cucumber & crème fraîche, cook the onion and garlic as above. Omit the flounder or sole. Add 13 oz skinned salmon, cut into chunks, and cook, stirring, for 1 minute. Add the wine, simmer as above, then add 1 tablespoon whole-grain mustard, the crème fraîche or Greek yogurt, and ¼ cucumber, peeled and sliced. Cook for 2 minutes, then stir in 1 tablespoon chopped dill instead of the mixed herbs.

split pea & bell pepper patties

Calories per serving **312**
Serves **4**
Preparation **20 minutes**, plus
cooling and chilling
Cooking time **45–50 minutes**

3 cups **Vegetable Stock** (see
page 48)
3 **garlic cloves**, unpeeled
1 ¼ cups **yellow split peas**,
well rinsed
olive oil spray
2 **red bell peppers**, cored,
seeded, and halved
1 **yellow bell pepper**, cored,
seeded, and halved
1 **red onion**, quartered
1 tablespoon chopped **mint**,
plus extra leaves to garnish
2 tablespoons **capers**, drained
and chopped
all-purpose flour, for dusting
salt and **black pepper**

Tzatziki
½ **cucumber**, finely chopped
1 **garlic clove**, crushed
2 tablespoons chopped **mint**
1 ¼ cups **low-fat plain yogurt**

Bring the stock to a boil in a large saucepan. Peel and halve 1 of the garlic cloves, then add to the pan with the split peas and cook for 40 minutes, until the split peas are tender. Drain, if necessary, then season with salt and black pepper and let cool slightly.

Meanwhile, lightly spray a roasting pan with oil. Put the remaining garlic cloves in the pan with the bell peppers and onion and roast in a preheated oven, at 400°F, for 20 minutes. When cool enough to handle, squeeze the roasted garlic cloves from their skins and chop with the roasted vegetables.

Mix together the split peas, vegetables, mint, and capers in a large bowl. Flour your hands and shape the mixture into 12 patties. Cover and chill until ready to cook.

Make the tzatziki by mixing the ingredients together in a bowl, cover, and chill for 30 minutes before serving.

Heat a skillet and spray with oil. Cook the patties, in batches if necessary, for 2 minutes on each side. Serve 3 patties per person, hot or cold, garnished with mint leaves, along with the tzatziki.

chicken tikka sticks & fennel raita

Calories per serving **179**
Serves **6**
Preparation time **20 minutes**,
  plus marinating and chilling
Cooking time **8–10 minutes**

1 **onion**, finely chopped
½–1 large **red** or **green chile**,
  seeded and finely chopped
  (to taste)
¾ inch piece of **fresh ginger
  root**, peeled and finely
  chopped
2 **garlic cloves**, finely chopped
⅔ cup **low-fat plain yogurt**
3 teaspoons **mild curry paste**
¼ cup chopped **cilantro**
4 **skinless, boneless chicken
  breasts** (about 5 oz each),
  cubed

Fennel raita
1 small **fennel bulb**
  (about 7 oz)
1 cup **low-fat plain yogurt**
3 tablespoons chopped
  cilantro
salt and **black pepper**

Mix together the onion, chile, ginger, and garlic in a nonmetallic dish. Add the yogurt, curry paste, and cilantro and stir together.

Add the cubed chicken to the yogurt mixture, mix to coat, cover, and let marinate in the refrigerator for at least 2 hours.

Make the raita. Cut the core away from the fennel and finely chop the remainder, including any green tops. Mix the fennel with the yogurt and cilantro and season with salt and black pepper. Spoon the raita into a serving dish, cover, and chill until needed.

Thread the chicken onto 12 bamboo skewers that have been soaked in water for at least 20 minutes and place them on an aluminum foil-lined broiler rack. Cook under a preheated broiler for 8–10 minutes, turning once, until browned and the chicken is cooked through. Serve 2 skewers per person with the raita.

For red pepper & almond chutney, to serve with the skewers instead of the raita, place 1 cup roasted red peppers in a blender or food processor with a handful of mint leaves, 1 chopped garlic clove, and ½ teaspoon chili powder. Blend until smooth, then add salt to taste and 1½ tablespoons toasted slivered almonds. Pulse a couple of times to coarsely crush the almonds, then stir in 1 tablespoon chopped cilantro.

turkey ragout

Calories per serving **190**
Serves **4**
Preparation time **10 minutes**
Cooking time **1 hour**
50 minutes

1 **turkey drumstick**
(about 1 1/4 lb)
2 **garlic cloves**, peeled
15 **pearl onions** or **shallots**,
peeled
3 **carrots**, diagonally sliced
1 1/4 cups **red wine**
a few **thyme sprigs**
2 **bay leaves**
2 tablespoons chopped
flat leaf parsley
1 teaspoon **port wine jelly**
1 teaspoon **whole-grain**
mustard
salt and **black pepper**

Remove the skin from the turkey drumstick and make a few cuts in the flesh. Finely slice 1 of the garlic cloves and push the slivers into the slashes. Crush the remaining garlic clove.

Transfer the drumstick to a large, flameproof casserole or roasting pan with the onions or shallots, carrots, crushed garlic, wine, thyme, and bay leaves. Season well with salt and black pepper, cover, and roast in a preheated oven, at 350°F, for about 1 3/4 hours or until the turkey is cooked through.

Remove the turkey and vegetables from the casserole or roasting pan and keep hot. Bring the pan juices to a boil on the stove, discarding the bay leaves. Add the parsley, jelly, and mustard and boil for 5 minutes, until slightly thickened. Season with salt and black pepper. Carve the turkey and serve with the vegetables and sauce in 4 bowls, accompanied by steamed new potatoes, if desired (remembering to count the extra calories).

For spicy roasted turkey with vegetables, prepare the turkey drumstick as above, then rub with the juice of 1 lemon and 2 tablespoons mild curry powder. Toss the pearl onions or shallots and chopped carrots in 2 tablespoons olive oil and place in a roasting pan with the turkey drumstick on top. Roast as above for 35 minutes, then add 2 cored, seeded, and chopped red bell peppers, 1 large sweet potato, chopped, and 1 large zucchini, thickly sliced. Baste the turkey with any juices and roast for another 1 hour or until the turkey drumstick is cooked through. Carve the turkey and serve with the vegetables and pan juices.

scallops with cilantro yogurt

Calories per serving **217**
Serves **2**
Preparation time **15 minutes**
Cooking time **5 minutes**

⅔ cup **low-fat plain yogurt**
2 tablespoons chopped
  cilantro
finely grated zest and juice
  of **1 lime**
2 teaspoons **sesame oil**
½ small **red onion**, finely
  chopped
2½ inch **fresh ginger root**,
  peeled and grated
1 **garlic clove**, crushed
2 teaspoons **granulated
  sugar**
2 teaspoons **dark soy sauce**
1 tablespoon **water**
1 pointed **green bell pepper**,
  cored, seeded, and
  thinly sliced
7 oz large **scallops**
arugula leaves, to serve

Mix together the yogurt, cilantro, and lime zest in a small bowl, then transfer to a serving dish.

Heat half of the oil in a small skillet and gently sauté the onion for 3 minutes, until softened. Remove the pan from the heat and add the ginger, garlic, sugar, soy sauce, measured water, and lime juice.

Brush a ridged grill pan with the remaining oil. Add the green bell pepper and scallops, cook the scallops for 1 minute on each side until cooked through, and the bell pepper for a little longer, if necessary.

Pile the bell pepper and scallops onto 2 serving plates with the arugula. Heat the soy glaze through and spoon it over the scallops. Serve with the yogurt sauce.

For squid & arugula salad with sweet soy glaze, omit the scallops and green bell pepper. Make the yogurt and cilantro sauce as above and set aside. Heat 1 teaspoon peanut oil in a large wok or skillet over high heat. Add 7 oz raw squid rings and stir-fry for 1 minute before adding the onion, ginger, and garlic. Cook, stirring, for another 1 minute, then add the sugar, soy sauce, water, and only 1 teaspoon sesame oil. Stir for 30 seconds, then remove from the heat and serve on a bed of arugula leaves with the yogurt and cilantro sauce on the side.

liver with garlic mashed potatoes

Calories per serving **393**
Serves **2**
Preparation time **10 minutes**
Cooking time **10–12 minutes**

3 **russet** or **Yukokn god**
   potatoes, cubed
1 **garlic clove**, peeled
3 tablespoons **low-fat crème**
   fraîche or **Greek yogurt**
½ tablespoon chopped **sage**,
   plus extra to garnish
1 tablespoon **all-purpose**
   flour
2 slices of **calf liver**
   (about 5 oz each)
1½ teaspoons **olive oil**
salt and **black pepper**
gravy, to serve

Cook the potatoes and garlic in a saucepan of lightly salted boiling water for 10–12 minutes, until tender, then drain. Return the potatoes and garlic to the pan and mash with the crème fraîche or yogurt and sage. Season well with black pepper.

Meanwhile, season the flour with salt and black pepper, then press the pieces of liver into the seasoned flour to coat them all over. Heat the oil in a skillet, add the liver, and cook for 1–2 minutes on each side or until cooked to your preference.

Serve the liver hot with the garlic mashed potatoes and gravy, garnished with extra chopped sage.

For liver with garlic lentils, heat 1 tablespoon olive oil in a saucepan and cook 1 diced carrot, 2 diced celery sticks, 2 finely chopped garlic cloves, and 1 diced onion for 3–4 minutes, until softened. Add 1 drained (15 oz) can green lentils or 2 cups cooked dried green lentils and cook for another 4–5 minutes. Meanwhile, cook the liver as above. Stir the chopped sage into the lentils and serve with the liver.

thai mussel curry with ginger

Calories per serving **230**
Serves **4**
Preparation time **30 minutes**
Cooking time **13 minutes**

½–1 large **red chile** (to taste)
2 **shallots**, quartered
1 **lemon grass stalk**
1 inch piece of **fresh ginger
root**, peeled and chopped
1 tablespoon **sunflower oil**
1⅔ cups **reduced-fat
coconut milk**
4–5 **kaffir lime leaves**
⅔ cup **fish stock**
2 teaspoons **Thai fish sauce**
3 lb **fresh mussels**, soaked
in cold water
1 small bunch of **cilantro**, torn
into pieces, to garnish

Halve the chile and keep the seeds for extra heat,
if desired. Put the chile, shallots, and lemon grass into
a blender or food processor with the ginger and blend
together until finely chopped.

Heat the oil in large, deep saucepan, add the finely
chopped ingredients, and sauté over medium heat for
5 minutes, stirring until softened. Add the coconut milk,
kaffir lime leaves, fish stock, and fish sauce and cook
for 3 minutes. Set aside.

Meanwhile, pick over the mussels and discard any that
are opened or have cracked shells. Scrub with a small
nailbrush, remove any barnacles, and pull off any small,
hairy beards. Put them in a bowl of clean water and set
aside until ready to cook.

Reheat the coconut milk mixture. Drain the mussels
and add to the mixture. Cover the pan with a lid and
cook for about 5 minutes, until the mussel shells
have opened.

Spoon the mussels and the coconut sauce into 4 bowls,
discarding any mussels that have not opened. Garnish
with the cilantro.

For Thai chicken & eggplant curry, prepare the
above recipe up to the end of the second step. Omit the
mussels. Pour in 1 cup chicken stock and bring to a boil.
Stir in 1 diced eggplant and 10 oz skinless, boneless
chicken breast, cut into large chunks. Bring to a boil
again, cover, and simmer for 12–15 minutes, until the
chicken is cooked through and the eggplant tender.
Serve with a sprinkling of cilantro.

pork skewers with coleslaw

Calories per serving **296**
Serves **4**
Preparation time **25 minutes**,
  plus marinating
Cooking time **7–10 minutes**

1 ¼ lb **lean pork loin**, cubed

Barbecue marinade
2 tablespoons packed **light
  brown sugar**
2 tablespoons **ketchup**
2 tablespoons **dark soy sauce**
1 teaspoon **Chinese five-
  spice powder**
2 tablespoons **orange juice**

Coleslaw
1 tablespoon **red wine vinegar**
2 teaspoons **piri-piri sauce** or
  marinade
½ teaspoon **granulated sugar**
¼–⅓ cup **extra-light
  mayonnaise**
½ **red cabbage**, shredded
2 **carrots**, grated
2 **scallions**, thinly sliced
salt and **black pepper**

Mix together all the marinade ingredients in a large, nonmetallic bowl until smooth. Add the pork and mix until well coated. Cover and let marinate at room temperature for 15 minutes.

Meanwhile, make the coleslaw. Mix together the vinegar, piri-piri sauce or marinade, sugar, and mayonnaise in a small bowl. Toss together the cabbage, carrots, and scallions in a large bowl, then add the dressing and mix together until well combined. Season with salt and black pepper and set aside.

Thread the pork onto 8 metal skewers and cook under a preheated broiler for 7–10 minutes, turning occasionally, until cooked through and sticky. Serve 2 skewers per person with the coleslaw and steamed white rice, if desired (remembering to count the extra calories).

For sweet & spicy pork wraps, cut the pork into strips. Mix together the marinade ingredients as above, add the pork, and mix until well coated. Cover and let marinate in the refrigerator for 30 minutes. Heat a ridged grill pan or heavy skillet until hot, add the pork, and cook for 6–8 minutes, turning frequently, until cooked through. Divide among 8 small flour tortillas. Cut 1 cucumber into thin matchsticks and divide among the tortillas along with 8 shredded scallions. Roll up each tortilla around the filling and serve.

lamb & bean stew

Calories per serving **288**
Serves **4**
Preparation time **5 minutes**
Cooking time **1 hour**
   20 minutes

1 teaspoon **olive oil**
11½ oz **lean lamb**, cubed
16 **pickling onions**, peeled
1 **garlic clove**, crushed
1 tablespoon **all-purpose**
  flour
2½ cups **lamb stock**
  (made with concentrated
  liquid stock)
¾ cup canned **diced**
  tomatoes
1 **bouquet garni**
3 cups canned **great Northern**
  beans, drained and rinsed
16 **cherry tomatoes**
black pepper

Heat the oil in a flameproof casserole or saucepan, add the lamb, and cook for 3–4 minutes, until browned all over. Remove the lamb from the casserole and set aside.

Add the onions and garlic to the pan and sauté for 4–5 minutes, until the onions are beginning to brown.

Return the lamb and any juices to the pan, then stir through the flour and add the stock, tomatoes, bouquet garni, and beans. Bring to a boil, stirring, then cover, reduce the heat, and simmer for 1 hour, until the lamb is just tender.

Add the cherry tomatoes to the dish and season well with black pepper. Simmer for another 10 minutes, then serve with steamed potatoes and green beans, if desired (remembering to count the extra calories).

For pork & cider stew, replace the lamb with 11½ oz lean pork tenderloin, cubed. Brown as above and set aside. Cook the onions and garlic as above, add the browned pork, and stir in the flour. Pour in 1⅔ cups each of ham stock and cider, instead of the lamb stock. Omit the canned tomatoes, and add the bouquet garni and beans. Simmer, covered, as above, adding 2 cups cubed carrots to the pan 30 minutes into cooking. Simmer for another 30 minutes, omitting the cherry tomatoes. Remove from the heat and stir in 2 tablespoons whole-grain mustard and a handful of chopped flat leaf parsley.

chermoula tofu & roasted veg

Calories per serving **241**
Serves **4**
Preparation time **15 minutes**
Cooking time **1 hour**

½ cup finely chopped **cilantro**
3 **garlic cloves**, chopped
1 teaspoon **cumin seeds**,
  lightly crushed
finely grated zest of **1 lemon**
½ teaspoon **dried red pepper
  flakes**
¼ cup **olive oil**
8 oz **tofu**
2 **red onions**, quartered
2 **zucchini**, thickly sliced
2 **red bell peppers**, cored,
  seeded, and sliced
2 **yellow bell peppers**, cored,
  seeded, and sliced
1 small **eggplant**,
  thickly sliced
salt

Mix together the cilantro, garlic, cumin, lemon zest, and red pepper flakes with 1 tablespoon of the oil and a little salt in a small bowl to make the chermoula.

Pat the tofu dry on paper towels and cut it in half. Cut each half horizontally into thin slices. Spread the chermoula generously over the slices. Set aside.

Sprinkle the vegetables in a roasting pan and drizzle with the remaining oil. Bake in a preheated oven, at 400°F, for about 45 minutes, until lightly browned, turning the ingredients once or twice during cooking.

Arrange the tofu slices over the vegetables, with the side spread with the chermoula uppermost, and bake for another 10–15 minutes, until the tofu is lightly browned.

For chermoula tuna with tomato & zucchini salad,
prepare the chermoula as above and rub it all over 4 fresh tuna steaks (about 4 oz each). Let marinate while you prepare the salad. Thinly slice 4 zucchini, using a vegetable peeler, then place in a bowl and toss with 1 tablespoon olive oil. Heat a large, nonstick skillet or ridged grill pan over high heat, add the zucchini strips, and cook for 1–2 minutes on each side until golden. Slice 4 beefsteak tomatoes and arrange on 4 plates with the cooked zucchini. Heat 2 tablespoons olive oil in the skillet or ridged grill pan, add the tuna, and cook for 1½ minutes on each side until browned on the outside but still pink in the center. Serve with the salad, with the pan juices poured over the top and lemon wedges for squeezing.

red snapper with baked tomatoes

Calories per serving **287**
Serves **4**
Preparation time **20 minutes**
Cooking time **18–20 minutes**

8 red snapper fillets
  (about 3½ oz each)
finely grated zest of **1 lemon**
2 teaspoons **baby capers**,
  drained
2 **scallions**, finely sliced
2½ cups mixed **red** and
  yellow cherry tomatoes
1½ cups trimmed
  green beans
2 **garlic cloves**, finely chopped
1 (2 oz) can **anchovy fillets**,
  drained and chopped
1 tablespoon **olive oil**
2 tablespoons **lemon juice**
salt and **black pepper**

To garnish
2 tablespoons chopped
  parsley
8 **caperberries**

Tear off 4 large sheets of aluminum foil and line with nonstick parchment paper. Place 2 fish fillets on each piece of parchment paper, then sprinkle with the lemon zest, capers, and scallions and season with salt and black pepper. Fold over the paper-lined foil and scrunch the edges together to seal. Place the packages on a large baking sheet.

Put the tomatoes in an ovenproof dish with the beans, garlic, anchovies, oil, and lemon juice. Season with salt and black pepper and mix well. Bake in a preheated oven, at 400°F, for 10 minutes, until the tomatoes and beans are tender.

Place the fish packages next to the vegetables in the oven and bake for another 8–10 minutes, until the flesh flakes easily when pressed in the center with a knife.

Spoon the vegetables onto 4 serving plates, then top each with 2 steamed fish fillets. Garnish with the chopped parsley and caperberries, and serve immediately.

For red snapper & tomato stew, heat 1 tablespoon olive oil in a saucepan, add the scallions and garlic along with 1 trimmed and sliced fennel bulb, and cook for 5 minutes, until just softened. Add the tomatoes and 1⅔ cups fish stock, bring to a simmer, and cook for 15 minutes. Add 4 red snapper fillets (about 3½ oz each), quartered, and 7 oz cooked, peeled shrimp and cook for 3–4 minutes, until the fish has turned opaque. Sprinkle in the chopped parsley and lemon juice, and serve with crusty bread.

lobster with shallots & vermouth

Calories per serving **275**
Serves **4**
Preparation time **1 hour**
Cooking time **10–11 minutes**

2 **cooked lobsters**
  (about 1¼–1½ lb each)
2 tablespoons **olive oil**
2 **shallots**, finely chopped
4 canned **anchovy fillets**,
  drained and finely chopped
⅓ cup **dry vermouth**
⅓ cup **low-fat crème fraîche**
  or **Greek yogurt**
2–4 teaspoons **lemon juice**
  (to taste)
black pepper

To garnish
paprika
arugula leaves

Lay one lobster on its back. Cut in half, beginning at the head, down through the line between the claws, unfurling the tail as you cut until the lobster can be separated into two. Repeat with the second lobster. Take out the black, threadlike intestine that runs down the tail and the small whitish sac in the top of the head. Leave the greeny liver.

Twist off the big claws. Crack these open with poultry shears, a nutcracker, pestle, or rolling pin. Peel away the shell and lift out the white meat, discarding the white, oval membrane in the center of the claw. Twist off the small claws, being careful not to tear off body meat, and discard.

Scoop out the thick, white tail meat, slice, and reserve it. Carefully remove the remaining lobster meat from the body, picking it over for stray pieces of shell and bone. Rinse the shells and put them on 4 serving plates.

Heat the oil in a large skillet, add the shallots, and sauté gently for 5 minutes, until softened and just beginning to brown. Mix in the anchovies, vermouth, and black pepper and cook for 2 minutes.

Add the lobster meat and crème fraîche or yogurt and heat for 3–4 minutes. Stir in the lemon juice. Spoon into the shells, sprinkle with paprika, and garnish with arugula.

For lobster & fennel salad, prepare the lobster flesh as above, cutting into large chunks, and then pan-fry in a hot skillet in 1 tablespoon olive oil. Let cool while you thinly slice 2 fennel bulbs and 3 celery sticks. Whisk together the juice of 1 lemon, ¼ cup olive oil, 1 teaspoon Dijon mustard, 2 chopped tarragon sprigs, and 1 crushed garlic clove. Toss with the lobster, fennel, and celery, and serve on a bed of salad greens.

chicken with spring vegetables

Calories per serving **370**
Serves **4**
Preparation time **15 minutes**,
    plus resting
Cooking time **about 1¼ hours**

3 lb **chicken**
about 6⅓ cups **chicken stock**
2 **shallots**, halved
2 **garlic cloves**, peeled
2 **parsley sprigs**
2 **marjoram sprigs**
2 **lemon thyme sprigs**
2 **carrots**, halved
1 **leek**, sliced
7 oz **baby broccoli**
8 oz **asparagus**, trimmed
½ **savoy cabbage**, shredded

Put the chicken in a large saucepan and pour over enough stock to just cover the chicken. Add the shallots, garlic, herbs, carrots, and leek to the pan and bring to a boil over medium-high heat, then reduce the heat and simmer gently for 1 hour or until the chicken is falling away from the bones.

Add the remaining vegetables to the pan and simmer for another 6–8 minutes, until the vegetables are cooked.

Turn off the heat and let rest for 5–10 minutes. Remove the skin from the chicken, then divide the chicken among 4 deep serving bowls with the vegetables, with spoonfuls of the broth ladled over the top. Serve with hunks of crusty bread, if desired (remembering to count the extra calories).

For broiled chicken with spring vegetables, cook 4 skinless, boneless chicken breasts (about 4 oz each), under a preheated broiler for 8–10 minutes on each side or until cooked through. Meanwhile, put the broccoli, asparagus, and savoy cabbage in the top of a steamer, cover, and cook for a few minutes, until just tender. Divide the vegetables among 4 warmed plates, top with the broiled and sliced chicken and sprinkle with chopped parsley and thyme, then drizzle lightly with extra virgin olive oil.

thai beef & mixed pepper stir-fry

Calories per serving **255**
Serves **4**
Preparation time **15 minutes**
Cooking time **8–10 minutes**

1 lb **lean tenderloin steak**
1 tablespoon **sesame oil**
1 **garlic clove**, finely chopped
1 **lemon grass stalk**, finely
 shredded
1 inch piece of **fresh ginger
 root**, peeled and finely
 chopped
1 **red bell pepper**, cored,
 seeded, and thickly sliced
1 **green bell pepper**, cored,
 seeded, and thickly sliced
1 **onion**, thickly sliced
2 tablespoons **lime juice**
black pepper
cilantro leaves, to garnish

Cut the beef across the grain into long, thin strips.

Heat the oil in a wok or large skillet over high heat. Add the garlic and stir-fry for 1 minute. Add the beef and stir-fry for 2–3 minutes, until lightly browned. Stir in the lemon grass and ginger and remove the pan from the heat. Remove the beef from the pan and set aside.

Add the bell peppers and onion to the pan and stir-fry for 2–3 minutes, until the onions are just turning golden brown and are slightly softened.

Return the beef to the pan, stir in the lime juice, and season to taste with black pepper. Serve garnished with cilantro leaves and accompanied by steamed white rice, if desired (remembering to count the extra calories).

For marinated tofu & vegetable stir-fry, replace the beef with 13 oz tofu, patted dry with paper towels and cut into strips. Mix together 3 tablespoons soy sauce, 2 teaspoons honey, and 1 teaspoon Dijon mustard in a bowl, add the tofu, and toss until well coated. Cover and let marinate for 30 minutes. Cook the stir-fry as above, adding the tofu at the end of cooking, along with ½ cup bean sprouts.

shrimp with tamarind & lime

Calories per serving **122**
Serves **6**
Preparation time **5 minutes**
Cooking time **10 minutes**

2 lb **jumbo shrimp** or **spiny
    lobster** in their shells
    (thawed if frozen)
2 tablespoons **olive oil**
1 large **onion**, chopped
3–4 **garlic cloves**, finely
    chopped
1½ inch piece of **fresh ginger
    root**, peeled and finely
    chopped
2 teaspoons **tamarind paste**
juice of **2 limes**
1¼ cups **fish stock**
1 small bunch of **cilantro**,
    torn into pieces, to garnish
lime wedges, to serve

Heat the oil in a large saucepan or wok, add the onion, and cook the shrimp for 5 minutes, until just beginning to brown.

Stir in the garlic, ginger, and tamarind paste, then mix in the lime juice and stock.

Bring the stock to a boil, add the shrimp, and cook, stirring, for 5 minutes, until the shrimp are bright pink. Spoon into 6 bowls and serve garnished with the torn cilantro leaves and lime wedges.

For shrimp with tomato & coconut, brown the onions as above. Add the shrimp, garlic, and ginger and cook until the shrimp turn pink, then add the lime juice, 2 teaspoons tamarind paste, ½ cup reduced-fat coconut milk, and 3 tomatoes, seeded and finely chopped. Omit the stock. Bring to a boil, then reduce the heat and simmer for 2 minutes. Serve with the cilantro and lime garnish.

wild mushroom stroganoff

Calories per serving **206**
Serves **4**
Preparation time **15 minutes**
Cooking time **15–16 minutes**

2 tablespoons **butter**
1 tablespoon **olive oil**
1 **onion**, sliced
6⅔ cups sliced **cremini mushrooms** (about 13 oz)
2 **garlic cloves**, finely chopped
2 teaspoons **paprika**, plus extra to garnish
⅓ cup **vodka**
1⅔ cups **Vegetable Stock** (see page 48)
generous pinch of **ground cinnamon**
generous pinch of **ground mace**
5 oz **wild mushrooms**, large ones sliced
⅓ cup **low-fat crème fraîche** or **sour cream**
salt and **black pepper**
chopped **parsley**, to garnish

Heat the butter and oil in a skillet, add the onion, and sauté for 5 minutes, until lightly browned. Stir in the cremini mushrooms and garlic and cook for 4 minutes. Stir in the paprika and cook for 1 minute.

Pour in the vodka. When it is bubbling, light with a match and stand back. Once the flames have subsided, stir in the stock, cinnamon, and mace and season with salt and black pepper. Simmer for 3–4 minutes.

Add the wild mushrooms and cook for 2 minutes. Stir in 2 tablespoons of the crème fraîche or sour cream.

Spoon the stroganoff onto 4 serving plates and top with spoonfuls of the remaining crème fraîche or sour cream, a sprinkling of paprika and a little parsley. Serve with sweet mashed potatoes, if desired (remembering to count the extra calories).

For wild mushroom risotto, heat the butter and olive oil in a skillet and sauté the chopped onion, and wild mushrooms for 4–5 minutes, until golden. Add the garlic and cook for 1 minute, then pour in ½ cup white wine and 1 cup risotto rice and stir well. Add up to 4 cups hot vegetable stock to the pan, one ladleful at a time, stirring and allowing the liquid to be absorbed before adding more, and cook for about 20 minutes, until the rice is al dente. Season with salt and black pepper and serve with a sprinkling of grated Parmesan cheese and chopped parsley.

scallops with white bean puree

Calories per serving **293**
Serves **4**
Preparation time **10 minutes**
Cooking time **20 minutes**

3⅓ cups canned **cannellini beans**, drained and rinsed
2 **garlic cloves**
1 cup **Vegetable Stock** (see page 48)
2 tablespoons chopped **parsley**
2 teaspoons **olive oil**
16 **baby leeks**
3 tablespoons **water**
16 large **scallops**
parsley sprigs, to garnish

Place the beans, garlic, and stock in a saucepan and bring to a boil, then reduce the heat and simmer for 10 minutes. Remove from the heat, drain off any excess liquid, then mash with a potato masher and stir in the parsley. Keep warm.

Heat half the oil in a nonstick skillet, add the leeks, and sauté for 2 minutes, then add the measured water. Cover and simmer for 5–6 minutes, until tender.

Meanwhile, heat the remaining oil in a small skillet, add the scallops, and cook for 1 minute on each side, until just cooked through. Serve with the white bean puree and leeks and garnish with parsley sprigs.

For prosciutto wrapped scallops with minty pea puree, make the puree as above, replacing the beans with 2 cups frozen and thawed peas, and using mint instead of parsley. Remove the fat from 8 slices of prosciutto and cut them in half widthwise. Wrap a strip of ham around each scallop and season with salt and black pepper. Omit the leeks. Heat all the oil in a large nonstick skillet, add the scallops, and cook for 2 minutes on each side, until just cooked through. Serve immediately with the pea puree.

lime & ginger shrimp coleslaw

Calories per serving **143**
Serves **2**
Preparation time **15 minutes**
Cooking time **2–3 minutes**

¼ **napa cabbage** or **pointed spring cabbage**, thinly shredded
1 **carrot**, coarsely grated
1 cup **bean sprouts**
½ small bunch of **cilantro**, finely chopped
1 **scallion**, thinly sliced
4 oz **peeled jumbo shrimp**
1 teaspoon **Chinese five-spice powder**
1½ teaspoons **peanut oil**
lime wedges, to serve

Dressing
1 teaspoon peeled and finely grated **fresh ginger root**
1 tablespoon **lime juice**
½ teaspoon packed **palm sugar** or **light brown sugar**
1 tablespoon **light soy sauce**
1½ teaspoons **peanut oil**

Toss together the cabbage, carrot, bean sprouts, cilantro, and scallion in a large bowl and set aside.

Make the dressing by placing all the ingredients in a screw-top jar, adding the lid, and shaking until well combined. Set aside.

Mix together the shrimp and Chinese five-spice powder in a bowl until the shrimp are well coated. Heat the oil in a wok or skillet over medium-high heat, add the shrimp, and stir-fry for 2–3 minutes, until they turn pink and are cooked through. Remove from the pan and drain on paper towels.

Pour the dressing over the vegetables and toss together, then pile the coleslaw on 2 serving plates. Sprinkle the shrimp over the top and serve with lime wedges.

For lime & ginger shrimp stir-fry, heat 1 tablespoon peanut oil in a wok or skillet over medium-high heat, add the ginger, Chinese five-spice powder, and scallion and stir-fry for 1 minute. Add the cabbage, carrot, and bean sprouts and stir-fry for 1–2 minutes, then stir in the shrimp and stir-fry as above. Toss with the lime juice, soy sauce, and chopped cilantro and serve immediately, with boiled rice, if desired.

spicy eggplant curry

Calories per serving **231**
Serves **4**
Preparation time **15 minutes**,
  plus cooling
Cooking time **20 minutes**

1 teaspoon **cumin seeds**
4 teaspoons **coriander seeds**
1 teaspoon **cayenne pepper**
2 **green chiles**, seeded and
  sliced
½ teaspoon **ground turmeric**
4 **garlic cloves**, crushed
1 inch piece of **fresh ginger
  root**, peeled and grated
1¼ cups **warm water**
1⅔ cups **reduced-fat
  coconut milk**
1 tablespoon **tamarind paste**
1 large **eggplant**, thinly sliced
  lengthwise
salt and **black pepper**
4 **mini plain naans** or **pita
  breads**, to serve

Dry-fry the cumin and coriander seeds in a small, nonstick skillet for a few minutes, until aromatic and toasted. Let cool, then crush together.

Mix together the crushed seeds, cayenne, chiles, turmeric, garlic, ginger, and the measured water in a large saucepan and simmer for 10 minutes, until thickened. Season with salt and black pepper, then stir in the coconut milk and tamarind paste.

Arrange the eggplant slices on an aluminum foil-lined broiler rack and brush the tops with some of the curry sauce. Cook under a preheated hot broiler until golden.

Stir the eggplant slices into the curry sauce. Serve hot with mini plain naan or pita breads.

asian steamed chicken salad

Calories per serving **273**
Serves **2**
Preparation time **15 minutes**,
   plus cooling
Cooking time **8–10 minutes**

2 **skinless, boneless chicken
   breasts** (about 5 oz each)
¼ small **napa cabbage**, finely
   shredded
½ **large carrot**, grated
1¼ cups **bean sprouts**
handful of **cilantro**,
   finely chopped
handful of **mint**, finely chopped
½ **red chile**, seeded and finely
   sliced (optional)

Dressing
3 tablespoons **sunflower oil**
juice of 1 **lime**
2 teaspoons **Thai fish sauce**
1½ tablespoons **light
   soy sauce**
1½ teaspoons peeled and
   finely chopped **fresh
   ginger root**

Put the chicken in the top of a steamer, cover, and
cook for about 8 minutes or until the chicken is cooked
through. Alternatively, poach the chicken in a saucepan
of simmering water for 8–10 minutes, until cooked
through and tender. Remove from the pan and let
stand until cool enough to handle.

Meanwhile, make the dressing by placing all the
ingredients in a screw-top jar, adding the lid, and
shaking until well combined.

Cut or tear the cooked chicken into strips and mix
with 1 tablespoon of the dressing in a bowl. Let
cool completely.

Toss together all the vegetables, herbs, and chile, if
using, in a large bowl, then divide between 2 serving
plates. Sprinkle the salad over the cold chicken and
serve immediately with the remaining dressing.

For Asian chicken stir-fry, heat 1 tablespoon
sunflower oil in a wok over high heat, add the
chicken, cut into strips, chile, and ginger and stir-fry for
2–3 minutes, until the chicken is browned. Add 1 carrot,
cut into matchsticks, and stir-fry for 1 minute, then add
the cabbage and bean sprouts and stir-fry for another
2 minutes. Toss in the lime juice, Thai fish sauce,
and soy sauce, then finally the chopped herbs. Serve
immediately, with boiled rice, if desired.

seafood zarzuela

Calories per serving **240**
Serves **4**
Preparation time **30 minutes**
Cooking time **25 minutes**

4 **tomatoes**
1 tablespoon **olive oil**
1 large **onion**, finely chopped
2 **garlic cloves**, finely chopped
½ teaspoon **pimentón**
(smoked paprika)
1 **red bell pepper**, cored,
seeded, and diced
1 cup **fish stock**
⅔ cup **dry white wine**
2 large pinches of **saffron
threads**
4 small **bay leaves**
1 lb **fresh mussels**, soaked
in cold water
7 oz **squid**, cleaned and
rinsed in cold water
12 oz **skinless cod loin**,
cubed
salt and **black pepper**

Put the tomatoes in a large saucepan or heatproof bowl and pour over enough boiling water to cover, then let stand for about 1 minute. Drain and cool in a bowl of ice-cold water, then drain again. Skin the tomatoes and coarsely chop the flesh.

Heat the oil in a large saucepan, add the onion, and sauté for 5 minutes, until softened and just beginning to brown. Stir in the garlic and pimentón and cook, stirring, for another 1 minute.

Stir in the tomatoes, red bell pepper, stock, wine, and saffron. Add the bay leaves, season with salt and black pepper, and bring to a boil. Cover and simmer gently for 10 minutes, then remove the pan from the heat and set aside.

Meanwhile, pick over the mussels and discard any that are opened or have cracked shells. Scrub with a small nailbrush, remove any barnacles, and pull off any small, hairy beards. Put them in a bowl of clean water and set aside until ready to cook. Separate the squid tubes from the tentacles, then slice the tubes.

Reheat the tomato sauce, if necessary, add the cod and the sliced squid, and cook for 2 minutes. Drain the mussels and add to the pan, cover, and cook for 4 minutes. Add the squid tentacles and cook for another 2 minutes, until the fish is cooked through and all the mussel shells have opened. Gently stir, then serve, discarding any mussels that have not opened.

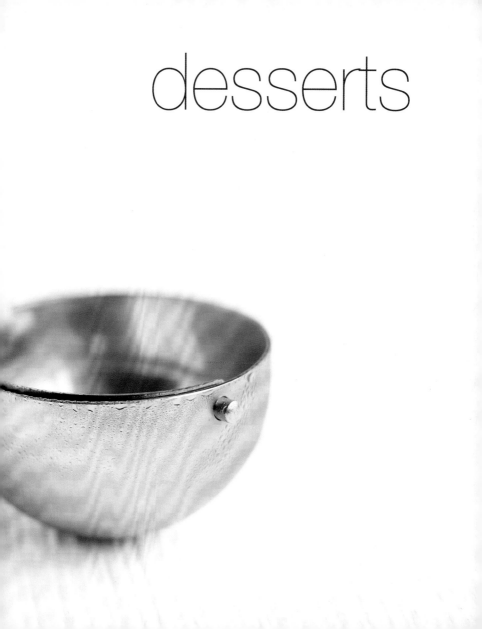

desserts

orangey baked nectarines

Calories per serving **161**
Serves **2**
Preparation time **10 minutes**
Cooking time **18–20 minutes**

2 tablespoons **orange liqueur**,
  such as Cointreau
½ teaspoon **vanilla bean
  paste** or **extract**
finely grated zest of ¼ **orange**
1 tablespoon **honey**
2 firm ripe **nectarines**, halved
  and pitted
⅓ cup **0% fat Greek yogurt
  with honey**, to serve

Put the liqueur, vanilla bean paste or extract, orange zest, and honey in a bowl and stir until well combined.

Arrange the nectarine halves, cut side up, in an ovenproof dish, then drizzle with the liqueur mixture. Bake in a preheated oven, at 350°F, for 18–20 minutes, until tender.

Divide the nectarines between 2 serving bowls and serve with the yogurt, drizzled with the pan juices.

For amaretti baked nectarines, arrange the nectarine halves in an ovenproof dish as above, then crumble 1 amaretti cookie into each one and drizzle each with 1 teaspoon maple syrup. Bake and then serve with the yogurt as above.

166

strawberry roulade

Calories per serving **177**
Serves **8**
Preparation time **30 minutes**,
  plus cooling
Cooking time **8 minutes**

3 **eggs**
⅔ cup **granulated sugar**
1 cup **all-purpose flour**, sifted
1 tablespoon **hot water**
1 lb fresh or frozen, thawed,
  drained and quartered
  strawberries, or 1 (15 oz)
  can **strawberries in natural
  juice**, drained and quartered
1 cup **fat-free natural
  fromage blanc** or **low-fat
  plain yogurt**
confectioners' sugar, for
  dusting

Lightly grease a 13 x 9 inch jellyroll pan. Line with a single sheet of wax paper to come about ½ inch above the sides of the pan. Lightly grease the paper.

Whisk the eggs and sugar in a large bowl over a saucepan of hot water until pale and thick. Fold the flour into the egg mixture with the measured water. Pour the batter into the prepared pan and bake in a preheated oven, at 425°F, for 8 minutes, until golden and set.

Meanwhile, place a sheet of wax paper 1 inch larger all around than the jellyroll pan on a clean, damp kitchen towel. Once cooked, immediately turn out the sponge face down on to the paper. Carefully peel off the lining paper. Roll the sponge up tightly with the new wax paper inside. Wrap the kitchen towel around the outside and place on a wire rack until cool, then unroll carefully.

Add half the strawberries to the fromage blanc or yogurt and spread over the sponge. Roll the sponge up again and trim the ends. Dust with confectioners' sugar and decorate with a few strawberries. Puree the remaining strawberries in a food processor or blender and serve as a sauce with the roll.

For vanilla & jelly roll, make the batter as above, folding in ½ teaspoon vanilla extract before baking. Bake, then roll, wrap, and cool as above. Lightly heat ½ cup raspberry jelly or jam and spread it over the sponge. Roll the sponge up again, trim the ends, and dust with confectioners' sugar.

caramel pear & marzipan tart

Calories per serving **268**

Serves **8**

Preparation time **10 minutes**, plus cooling

Cooking time **45 minutes**

4 tablespoons **unsalted butter**

¼ cup firmly packed **light brown sugar**

1 oz **marzipan**

6 ripe **pears**, peeled, halved, and cored

1 sheet **rolled dough pie crust**, thawed if frozen

Put the butter and sugar into a 9 inch cake pan. Put over medium heat and cook for about 5 minutes, stirring continuously, until golden. Remove from the heat.

Stuff a little marzipan into the cavity of each pear half, then carefully arrange them, cut side up, in the pan.

Roll out the dough on a lightly floured surface to the size of the pan, then place over the top of the pears and press down all around them. Bake in a preheated oven, at 375°F, for about 40 minutes, until the pastry is golden and the juices are bubbling.

Let cool in the pan for 10 minutes, then invert onto a large plate, cut into 8 wedges, and serve with a little ice cream, if desired (remembering to count the extra calories).

For pear, blackberry & marzipan tart, roll out the dough as above and put it onto a baking sheet. Core and chop 4 pears and combine in a bowl with the light brown sugar, marzipan, and 1 cup blackberries. Omit the butter. Place the fruit in the center of the dough circle, leaving a 2 inch rim, then lift the rim up over the edges of the fruit to make a tart. Brush the pastry with 1 tablespoon skim milk and dust with 1 tablespoon granulated sugar. Bake as above and serve warm.

ricotta, plum & almond cake

Calories per serving **150**
Serves **6**
Preparation time **30 minutes**,
  plus cooling and chilling
Cooking time **35–40 minutes**

8 sweet, ripe **red plums**
  (about 1 lb), pitted and
  quartered
1 cup **ricotta cheese**
¼–⅓ cup **granulated
  sweetener**
3 **eggs**, separated
¼ teaspoon **almond extract**
4 teaspoons **slivered
  almonds**
2 tablespoons **water**
1 tablespoon **confectioners'
  sugar**, sifted

Arrange half the plums randomly in an 8 inch springform pan with a bottom that has been greased and lined with parchment paper.

Mix together the ricotta, ¼ cup of the sweetener, the egg yolks, and almond extract in a bowl until smooth.

Whisk the egg whites in a second clean bowl until stiff peaks form. Fold into the ricotta mixture, then spoon it over the plums. Sprinkle with the slivered almonds and bake in a preheated oven, at 325°F, for 30–35 minutes, until the cake is risen, golden, and the center is just set. Check after 20 minutes and cover the top with aluminum foil if the almonds are browning too quickly.

Turn off the oven and let the cake cool with the door ajar for 15 minutes, then chill well.

Meanwhile, cook the remaining plums with the measured water in a covered saucepan for 5 minutes, until soft. Puree until smooth, mix in the remaining sweetener, if needed, then pour into a small bowl.

Remove the pan and lining paper and transfer the cake to a serving plate. Dust the top with the confectioners' sugar and serve, cut into 6 wedges, with the sauce.

For roasted almond plums with honeyed ricotta, mix together ¼ cup oats and 2 tablespoons all-purpose flour in a bowl, add 3 tablespoons diced butter, and rub in with the fingertips until resembling bread crumbs. Stir in 1½ teaspoons packed light brown sugar and the slivered almonds. Place the plums in a baking sheet and spoon the crumb topping over the top of each. Bake in a preheated oven, at 400°F, for 12–15 minutes. Serve with a dollop of ricotta and a drizzle of honey.

chocolate & chestnut roulade

Calories per serving **215**
Serves **8**
Preparation time **15 minutes**,
  plus cooling and chilling
Cooking time **20 minutes**

6 **eggs**, separated
⅔ cup **granulated sugar**
2 tablespoons **unsweetened cocoa powder**
⅓ cup **heavy cream**
¾ cup **chestnut puree** or **sweetened chestnut spread**
confectioners' sugar,
  for dusting

Grease and line an 11½ x 7 inch jellyroll pan. Whisk the egg whites in a large clean bowl until they form soft peaks. Put the egg yolks and sugar in a separate bowl and whisk together until thick and pale. Fold in the cocoa powder and the egg whites, then transfer to the prepared pan.

Bake in a preheated oven, at 350°F, for 20 minutes. Let cool in the pan, then turn out onto a piece of wax paper that has been dusted with confectioners' sugar.

Pour the cream into a large, clean bowl and whisk until it forms soft peaks. Fold the chestnut puree or spread into the cream, then smooth the mixture over the roulade.

Using the wax paper to help you, carefully roll up the roulade from one short end and lift it gently on to a serving dish (do not worry if it cracks). Dust with confectioners' sugar. Chill until needed and eat on the day it is made.

For chocolate orange roulade, prepare and bake the sponge cake as above. Whip the cream for the filling, then fold in 1 tablespoon marmalade and the finely grated zest of 1 orange. Omit the chestnut puree or spread. Spread the filling over the cake and roll up as above. Serve dusted with sifted confectioners' sugar.

white chocolate mousse

Calories per serving **202**
Serves **8**
Preparation time **15 minutes**,
  plus chilling

7 oz **white chocolate**,
  chopped
¼ cup **skim milk**
12 **cardamom pods**
7 oz **silken tofu**
¼ cup **granulated sugar**
1 **egg white**
1 cup **low-fat crème fraîche**
  or **Greek yogurt**, to serve
unsweetened cocoa powder,
  for dusting

Put the chocolate and milk in a heatproof bowl and melt over a saucepan of gently simmering water. To release the cardamom seeds, crush the pods using a mortar and pestle. Discard the pods and crush the seeds finely.

Place the cardamom pods and tofu in a food processor with half of the sugar and blend well to a smooth paste. Turn the mixture into a large bowl.

Whisk the egg white in a thoroughly clean bowl until it forms peaks. Gradually whisk in the remaining sugar.

Beat the melted chocolate mixture into the tofu mixture until completely combined. Using a large metal spoon, fold in the egg white. Spoon the mousse into 8 small coffee cups or glasses and chill for at least 1 hour. Serve topped with spoonfuls of crème fraîche or yogurt and a light dusting of cocoa powder.

For white chocolate & amaretto desserts, make the mousse mixture as above, omitting the cardamom and adding 2 tablespoons amaretto when blending the tofu. Complete the recipe and chill as above. Serve with fresh raspberries instead of the crème fraîche and cocoa.

passion fruit panna cotta

Calories per serving **144**
Serves **2**
Preparation time **15 minutes,**
plus cooling and chilling
Cooking time **5 minutes**

1 sheet of **gelatin**
4 **passion fruit**
½ cup **reduced-fat crème fraîche** (or increase the Greek yogurt to ¾ cup)
¼ cup **0% fat Greek yogurt**
¼ cup **water**
½ teaspoon **granulated sugar**
½ **vanilla bean**, split lengthwise

Soak the sheet of gelatin in a bowl of cold water for a few minutes, until softened.

Meanwhile, working over a bowl to catch the juice, halve the passion fruit, remove the seeds, and reserve for decoration. Mix the crème fraîche and yogurt into the passion fruit juice in the bowl.

Put the measured water into a saucepan with the sugar. Scrape the seeds from the vanilla bean into the pan, then heat gently, stirring, until the sugar has dissolved.

Drain the gelatin and add to the pan, then let cool.

Mix the gelatin mixture into the crème fraîche mixture, then pour into 2 ramekins or molds. Cover and chill for 6 hours or until set. Turn the panna cotta out of the ramekins or molds onto serving plates by briefly immersing their bottoms in hot water. Spoon the reserved passion fruit seeds over the top and serve.

chocolate & raspberry souffles

Calories per serving **287**
Serves **4**
Preparation time **10 minutes**
Cooking time **15–18 minutes**

3½ oz **semisweet chocolate**,
   broken into squares
3 **eggs**, separated
⅓ cup **all-purpose flour**,
   sifted
¼ teaspoon **baking powder**
⅓ cup **superfine sugar**
1 cup **raspberries**
confectioners' sugar, for
   dusting

Put the chocolate in a heatproof bowl and melt over a saucepan of gently simmering water.

Place the melted chocolate in a large bowl and whisk in the egg yolks. Fold in the flour and baking powder.

Whisk the egg whites and superfine sugar in a medium clean bowl until they form soft peaks. Beat a spoonful of the egg whites into the chocolate mixture to loosen it up before gently folding in the rest.

Divide the raspberries among 4 lightly greased ramekins, pour the chocolate mixture over them, then bake in a preheated oven, at 375°F, for 12–15 minutes, until the souffles have risen.

Dust with confectioners' sugar and serve immediately.

For chocolate & coffee souffles, stir 2 teaspoons instant coffee granules into the hot melted chocolate until it dissolves. Bake the souffles as above, omitting the raspberries. Make a cappuccino cream to serve with the souffles by folding 2 tablespoons sweetened strong black coffee into ½ cup low-fat crème fraîche or Greek yogurt. Serve the souffles straight out of the oven with a dollop of the cream.

brûlée vanilla cheesecake

Calories per serving **160**
Serves **8**
Preparation time **30 minutes**,
  plus cooling and chilling
Cooking time **30–35 minutes**

butter, for greasing
3 cups **low-fat cream cheese**
⅓ cup **granulated sweetener**
1½ teaspoons **vanilla extract**
finely grated zest of ½ **orange**
4 **eggs**, separated
1 tablespoon **confectioners'
  sugar**, sifted
3 **oranges**, peeled and cut
  into segments, to serve

Lightly grease an 8 inch springform pan. Mix together the cream cheese, sweetener, vanilla extract, orange zest, and egg yolks in a bowl until smooth.

Whisk the egg whites in a clean large bowl until soft peaks form, then fold a large spoonful into the cheese mixture to loosen it. Add the remaining egg whites and fold them in gently.

Pour the mixture into the prepared pan and level the surface. Bake in a preheated oven, at 325°F, for 30–35 minutes, until well risen, golden brown, and just set in the center.

Turn off the oven and let the cheesecake cool inside it for 15 minutes with the door slightly ajar. Remove from the oven, let cool, then chill for 4 hours. (The cheesecake will sink slightly as it cools.)

Run a knife around the cheesecake, loosen the pan, and transfer to a serving plate. Dust the top with the confectioners' sugar and caramelize the sugar with a cook's blowtorch. Serve within 30 minutes, while the sugar topping is still hard and brittle. Cut into 8 wedges and arrange on plates with the orange segments.

For lemon drizzle cheesecake, make the cheesecake as above, using the finely grated zest of 1 lemon in place of the orange zest. When the cheesecake has been chilled and removed from the pan, mix 3 tablespoons sifted confectioners' sugar with enough juice squeezed from the lemon to create a runny syrup. Spoon it over the cheesecake and sprinkle with the grated zest of another lemon.

orange, rhubarb & ginger slump

Calories per serving **256**
Serves **6**
Preparation time **10 minutes**
Cooking time **20–25 minutes**

1 ½ lb **rhubarb**, chopped into
  ¾ inch pieces
½ teaspoon **ground ginger**
grated rind and juice of
  1 orange
¼ cup **granulated sugar**
¼ cup **reduced-fat**
  mascarpone cheese
1 ⅓ cups **all-purpose flour**,
  sifted
1 ¼ teaspoons baking powder
4 tablespoons **unsalted**
  butter, cut into small pieces
grated zest of ½ **lemon**
⅓ cup **skim milk**

Put the rhubarb, ginger, orange zest and juice, and half the sugar in a saucepan. Bring to a boil, then reduce the heat and simmer gently for 5–6 minutes, until the rhubarb is just tender.

Transfer the rhubarb to an ovenproof dish and spoon over dollops of mascarpone.

Put the flour and baking powder into a bowl. Add the butter and rub in with the fingertips until the mixture resembles fine bread crumbs. Quickly stir through the remaining sugar, the lemon zest, and milk until combined. Place spoonfuls of the mixture over the rhubarb and mascarpone.

Bake in a preheated oven, at 400°F, for 12–15 minutes, until golden and bubbling. Serve with low-fat ice cream, if desired (remembering to count the extra calories).

For plum & apple slump, replace the rhubarb with 8 plums, pitted and cut into ¾ inch pieces, and 1 crisp, sweet apple, cored and cubed. Cook with the ginger, sugar, and orange until just tender, then transfer to an ovenproof dish. Spoon with ¼ cup low-fat (crème fraîche or Greek yogurt instead of the mascarpone, then continue as above.

champagne granita

Calories per serving **80**

Serves **6**

Preparation time **25 minutes**, plus cooling and freezing

⅓ cup firmly packed **light brown sugar**
⅔ cup **boiling water**
1½ cups **medium-dry champagne**
1 cup **raspberries**

Stir the sugar into the measured water until it has dissolved, then let cool.

Mix together the sugar syrup and champagne. Pour it into a shallow, nonstick baking pan so that it is no more than 1 inch deep.

Freeze the mixture for 2 hours, until it is mushy, then break up the ice crystals with a fork. Return the mixture to the freezer for an additional 2 hours, beating every 30 minutes, until it has formed fine, icy flakes.

Spoon the granita into 6 elegant glasses and top with the raspberries.

For pink grapefruit & ginger granita, grate a 1 inch piece of peeled fresh ginger root into a boiling water and sugar and stir until the sugar has dissolved. Set aside for 30 minutes before mixing the ginger sugar syrup into 1½ cups fresh pink grapefruit juice instead of the champagne. Complete the recipe as above, omitting the raspberries.

rhubarb & ginger parfait

Calories per serving **110**
Serves **6**
Preparation time **20 minutes**,
plus soaking, cooling and
chilling
Cooking time **8–9 minutes**

8 stalks **trimmed
rhubarb**, sliced
1 inch piece of **fresh ginger
root**, peeled and finely
chopped
⅓ cup **water**
3 teaspoons **powdered
gelatin**
4 **egg yolks**
⅓ cup **granulated sweetener**
1 cup **skim milk**
2 **egg whites**
½ cup **low-fat crème fraîche**
or **Greek yogurt**
a few drops of **pink food
coloring** (optional)
orange zest, to decorate

Put the rhubarb pieces in a saucepan with the ginger
and 2 tablespoons of the water. Cover and simmer for
5 minutes, until tender yet still bright pink. Mash or puree.

Put the remaining water in a small bowl and sprinkle
with the gelatin, making sure that all the powder is
absorbed by the water. Let soak for 5 minutes.

Whisk the egg yolks and sweetener until just mixed.
Pour the milk into a small saucepan and bring just to a
boil. Gradually whisk the milk into the egg yolks, then
pour the mixture back into the saucepan. Slowly bring
the custard almost to a boil, stirring continuously, until it
coats the back of the spoon. Do not let the custard boil
or the eggs will curdle.

Remove the pan from the heat and stir in the gelatin
until it has dissolved. Pour into a bowl, stir in the cooked
rhubarb, and let cool.

Whisk the egg whites until stiff, moist peaks form. Fold
the crème fraîche or yogurt and a few drops of coloring,
if used, into the cooled custard, then fold in the whisked
whites. Spoon into 6 glasses and chill for 4 hours until
lightly set. Decorate with orange zest to serve.

For rhubarb & ginger crisps, cook the rhubarb and
ginger as above, adding 3 tablespoons of the sweetener,
but do not mash or puree. Divide among 4 ramekins
on a baking sheet. Sift 1⅓ cups all-purpose flour into
a bowl, add 6 tablespoons diced butter, and rub in until
resembling bread crumbs. Stir in 2 tablespoons packed
dark brown sugar and the grated zest of 1 orange.
Sprinkle it over the rhubarb, then bake in a preheated
oven, at 375°F, for 20–25 minutes, until golden.

cherry & nectarine meringue

Calories per serving **245**

Serves **6**

Preparation time **20 minutes**, plus cooling

Cooking time **1 hour**

3 **egg whites**

¾ cup plus 2 tablespoons **superfine sugar**

1 teaspoon **strong black coffee**

1 cup **fat-free fromage blanc** or **Greek yogurt**

1 cup **cherries**

1 **nectarine**, pitted and sliced

Whisk the egg whites in a clean bowl until they form stiff peaks. Fold in 1 tablespoon of the sugar, then gradually whisk in the remainder. The meringue must be glossy and form peaks when spoonfuls are dropped into the bowl. Fold in the black coffee.

Line a baking sheet with a large sheet of parchment paper and spread the meringue mixture over the paper to form an 8 inch diameter circle. Make a slight hollow in the center of the meringue and cook in a preheated oven, at 250°F, for 1 hour until the meringue is crisp. Remove from the oven and let cool for 10 minutes before peeling off the paper.

When the meringue is cold, fill the hollow in the top with the fromage blanc or yogurt. Arrange the cherries and nectarines chunks on top and serve immediately.

For berry & rosewater pavlova, make the meringue mixture as above, folding in ¼ teaspoon rosewater before placing it on the baking sheet and baking as above. Combine 1¾ cups mixed fresh berries (such as strawberries, raspberries, and blueberries) and stir in the zest and juice of ½ lemon. Use instead of the cherries and nectarines as a topping over the fromage blanc or yogurt.

apple & berry strudels

Calories per serving **102**
Serves **4**
Preparation time **15 minutes**
Cooking time **20 minutes**

2 **Granny smith** or **other cooking apples**, peeled and grated
1 ¼ cups **mixed berries**, plus extra to decorate
pinch of **ground cinnamon**
1 tablespoon **honey**
2 sheets of **phyllo pastry**
1 **egg white**, lightly beaten
mint sprigs, to decorate

Put the grated apples, berries, cinnamon, and 1 teaspoon of the honey in a saucepan and cook gently for about 5 minutes or until the fruit is soft.

Brush the phyllo pastry sheets with the egg white and place 1 sheet on top of the other. Cut the sheets into quarters and place one-quarter of the fruit in the center of each rectangle. Tuck in the ends of the pastry and roll into log shapes.

Place the strudels on a baking sheet, brush with the remaining honey, and bake in a preheated oven, at 300°F, for 15 minutes or until golden.

Decorate the strudels with mint sprigs and extra berries and serve with a little low-fat ice cream, if deisred (remembering to count the extra calories).

For summer apple & berry tarts, cook the fruit as above. Cut each phyllo pastry sheet into 8 squares. Melt 1 ½ tablespoons unsalted butter in a saucepan. Brush each phyllo square with melted butter, then lay one square on top of a second, at a slight angle to the first. Place each double layer of phyllo in a hole of a muffin pan to make 8 tart shells. Spoon the cooked fruit into the pastry shells and bake as above for 12–15 minutes, until the pastry edges are golden. Decorate and serve as above.

blueberry & mascarpone desserts

Calories per serving **146**

Serves **4**

Preparation time **15 minutes**,
  plus soaking and chilling

1½ cups **blueberries**

2 tablespoons **kirsch** or **vodka**

⅔ cup **reduced-fat
  mascarpone cheese**

⅔ cup **low-fat plain yogurt**

2 tablespoons **granulated
  sweetener**

grated zest and juice of **1 lime**

Combine 1 cup of the blueberries with the alcohol
in a bowl and let soak for at least 1 hour. Then mash
the blueberries.

Beat together the mascarpone and yogurt in a separate
bowl until smooth, then mix in the sweetener and the
lime zest and juice.

Layer alternate spoonfuls of mashed blueberries
and mascarpone in 4 glasses. Top with the whole
blueberries and chill until ready to serve.

For mango desserts with ricotta, replace the
blueberries with 1 peeled, pitted, and cubed fresh
mango and soak in 2 tablespoons vodka. To make the
cream, replace the mascarpone with ¾ cup ricotta
cheese and fold into the yogurt with 2 tablespoons
honey instead of the granular sweetener. Add the lime
zest and juice, then assemble the desserts as above.

mango & passion fruit brûlées

Calories per serving **131**
Serves **2**
Preparation time **10 minutes**,
  plus cooling and chilling
Cooking time **1–2 minutes**

½ **small mango**, pitted,
  peeled, and thinly sliced
1 **passion fruit**, halved and
  flesh scooped out
⅔ cup **low-fat plain yogurt**
½ cup **low-fat crème fraîche**
  or **Greek yogurt**
1½ teaspoons **confectioners'
  sugar**
a few drops of **vanilla extract**
1 tablespoon **demerara sugar**

Divide the mango between 2 ramekins. Mix together the passion fruit flesh, plain yogurt, crème fraîche or Greek yogurt, confectioners' sugar, and vanilla extract in a bowl, then spoon the mixture over the mango. Tap each ramekin to level the surface.

Sprinkle with the demerara sugar, then place the brûlées under a preheated hot broiler and cook for 1–2 minutes, until the sugar has melted. Let cool, then chill for about 30 minutes before serving.

For mango & passion fruit whips, puree the flesh of 1 mango in a blender or food processor and transfer to a bowl. Alternatively, rub the mango through a strainer to puree. Strain the pulp from 2 passion fruits to remove the seeds. Stir the passion fruit pulp into the mango puree, then stir in 1 cup 0% fat Greek yogurt. Spoon into 2 glasses and serve with lime wedges.

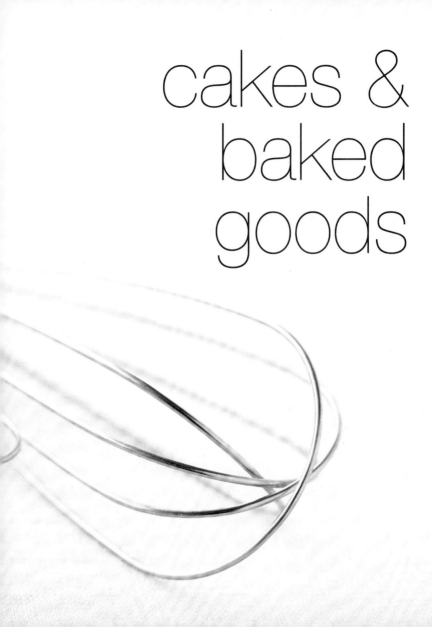

cakes & baked goods

lemon & raspberry cupcakes

Calories per cupcake **206**
Makes **12**
Preparation time **10 minutes**
Cooking time **12–15 minutes**

1 ¼ sticks **butter**, softened
¾ cup **granulated sugar**
½ cup **rice flour**
⅔ cup **cornstarch**
1 tablespoon **baking powder**
grated zest and juice of
   1 **lemon**
3 **eggs**, beaten
1 cup **raspberries**
1 tablespoon **lemon curd**

Line a large 12-section muffin pan with large paper muffin liners. Put all the ingredients except the raspberries and lemon curd into a large bowl and beat together using an electric handheld mixer, or beat with a wooden spoon. Fold in the raspberries.

Spoon half of the batter into the paper liners, dab with a little lemon curd, then add the remaining batter.

Bake the muffins in a preheated oven, at 400°F, for 12–15 minutes, until golden and firm to the touch. Transfer to a wire rack to cool.

For chocolate & banana cupcakes, make the cupcake batter as above, replacing the raspberries with the chopped flesh of 1 ripe banana. Spoon half the batter into the paper liners, then top with a small dollop of chocolate spread instead of the lemon curd. You will need about 1 tablespoon of spread in total. Top with the remaining batter and cook as above.

black currant & almond muffins

Calories per muffin **153**
Makes **12**
Preparation time **5 minutes**
Cooking time **20–25 minutes**

1⅔ cups **all-purpose flour**
2 teaspoons **baking powder**
½ teaspoon **baking soda**
pinch of **salt**
¼ cup **granulated sugar**
a few drops of **almond extract**
6 tablespoons **unsalted butter**, melted
1 cup **buttermilk**
10 oz canned **black currants or blueberries in natural juice**, drained, or 1¾ cups fresh **black currants or blueberries**
⅓ cup **slivered almonds**

Line a 12-section muffin pan with paper muffin liners. Sift the flour, baking powder, baking soda, and salt into a bowl, then stir in the sugar.

Mix together the almond extract, melted butter, buttermilk and black currants or blueberries in a separate large bowl, then lightly stir in the dry ingredients. The batter should still look a little lumpy.

Spoon the batter into the paper liners, sprinkle with the slivered almonds, then bake in a preheated oven, at 375°F, for 20–25 minutes, until risen and golden. Transfer to a wire rack to cool.

For raspberry & coconut muffins, make the muffin batter as above, omitting the almond extract and replacing the black currants with 2 cups fresh raspberries. Spoon into the muffin pan, omit the slivered almonds, and bake as above. Meanwhile, combine 2 tablespoons unsweetened dried coconut and 1 teaspoon granulated sugar in a bowl with 1 tablespoon boiling water. Spoon the coconut mixture over the muffins when they come out of the oven, then cool on a wire rack.

chocolate mini muffins

Calories per muffin **71**
Makes **40**
Preparation time **30 minutes**,
  plus cooling
Cooking time **15 minutes**

1¼ cups **brown rice flour**
2 tablespoons **chickpea/
  besan flour**
1 teaspoon **baking soda**
2 teaspoons **baking powder**
½ teaspoon **xanthan gum**
⅔ cup **granulated sugar**
6 tablespoons **butter**, melted
1 **egg**, beaten
1 cup **buttermilk**
⅓ cup **milk chocolate chips**
  or 3 oz **milk chocolate**,
  chopped
3 oz **milk chocolate**,
  to decorate

Line four 12-section mini-muffin pans with 40 paper liners. Sift the flours, baking soda, baking powder, and xanthan gum into a large bowl, then stir in the sugar.

Mix together the melted butter, egg, and buttermilk in a separate bowl. Gently combine the dry and wet ingredients, then lightly fold the milk chocolate chips or chopped milk chocolate into the batter, stirring well.

Spoon the batter into the paper liners and bake in a preheated oven, at 400°F, for 15 minutes, until golden and risen. Transfer to a wire rack to cool.

Put the remaining milk chocolate in a heatproof bowl and melt over a saucepan of gently simmering water. Drizzle it over the cooled muffins before serving.

For chocolate & orange mini muffins, make the muffin batter as above, replacing the milk chocolate chips with 2 tablespoons unsweetened cocoa powder. Coarsely chop ¼ cup candied orange peel and fold into the batter before baking as above.

banana & toffee bites

Calories per bite **122**
Makes **24**
Preparation time **10 minutes**,
  plus cooling
Cooking time **10–12 minutes**

1¼ cups **brown rice flour**
6 tablespoons **butter**,
  softened
⅓ cup **granulated sugar**
2 teaspoons **baking powder**
1 large **banana**, mashed
2 **eggs**
6 **toffees**, chopped

Topping
1 tablespoon packed **light
  brown sugar**
2 tablespoons **chewy
  banana slices** or
  dried banana chips

Line two 12-section mini muffin pans with paper liners. Put all the cake ingredients except the toffees into a food processor and blend until smooth, or beat in a large bowl. Stir in the toffees.

Spoon the batter into the paper liners, sprinkle with most of the brown sugar, and bake in a preheated oven, at 400°F, for 10–12 minutes, until golden and just firm to the touch. Transfer to a wire rack to cool.

Top the cooled cakes with chewy banana slices or banana chips and sprinkle with the remaining sugar.

For butterfly banana & walnut mini muffins, make the muffin batter as above, replacing the toffees with ½ cup coarsely chopped walnuts. Bake as above, then push 2 banana chip halves into each muffin, to look like butterfly wings. Serve with a light dusting of confectioners' sugar instead of the brown sugar.

scrumptious strawberry scones

Calories per scone **292**

Makes **8**

Preparation time **10 minutes**, plus cooling

Cooking time **12 minutes**

1 cup **rice flour**

⅔ cup **potato flour**

1 teaspoon **xanthan gum**

1 teaspoon **baking powder**

1 teaspoon **baking soda**

6 tablespoons **butter**, cubed

⅓ cup **granulated sugar**

1 extra-large **egg**, beaten

3 tablespoons **buttermilk**, plus a little extra for brushing

⅔ cup **heavy cream**

8 oz **strawberries**, lightly crushed

Put the flours, xanthan gum, baking powder, baking soda, and butter into a food processor and blend until the mixture resembles fine bread crumbs, or rub in by hand in a large bowl.

Stir in the sugar. Using the blade of a knife, stir in the egg and buttermilk until the dough comes together.

Transfer the dough onto a lightly floured surface and gently press it down to a thickness of 1 inch. Using a 2 inch cutter, cut out 8 circles.

Place on a lightly floured baking sheet, brush with a little buttermilk, then bake in a preheated oven, at 425°F, for about 12 minutes, until golden and risen. Transfer to a wire rack to cool.

Meanwhile, whisk the cream until it forms firm peaks and fold in the strawberries. Slice the scones in half and fill with the strawberry cream.

For raisin scones with blueberry cream, make the scones as above, adding ⅓ cup raisins to the raw dough before shaping. Bake and cool as above. Omit the cream and strawberries. Fold 3 tablespoons blueberry compote into ⅔ cup fat-free fromage blanc or Greek yogurt and use to fill the scones.

fruity mango oatmeal bars

Calories per flapjack **219**
Makes **12**
Preparation time **10 minutes**
Cooking time **35 minutes**

½ cup firmly packed **light
    brown sugar**
1 ¼ sticks **butter**
2 tablespoons **light
    corn syrup**
2 cups **millet flakes**
2 tablespoons **mixed seeds,**
    such as pumpkin and
    sunflower
½ cup coarsely chopped
    dried mango

Put the sugar, butte,r and syrup into a heavy saucepan and heat until melted, then stir in the remaining ingredients.

Spoon the batter into an 11 x 7 inch nonstick baking pan, press down lightly, and bake in a preheated oven, at 300°F, for 30 minutes.

Mark into 12 pieces, then cool before removing from the pan. Cut or break into 12 pieces once cooled.

For honey & ginger oatmeal bars, put ¼ cup firmly packed light brown sugar into a saucepan with ¼ cup honey and the butter. Omit the light corn syrup. Heat until melted, then add the millet flakes or 2 cups rolled oats and the seeds. Instead of the dried mango, stir in 1 piece of preserved ginger, finely chopped. Spoon the batter into the pan and continue as above.

apricot, fig & mixed seed bites

Calories per bite **107**
Makes **24**
Preparation time **10 minutes**
Cooking time **10–15 minutes**

⅔ cup **polyunsaturated margarine**
⅓ cup firmly packed **light brown sugar**
1 **egg**, beaten
2 tablespoons **water**
⅔ cup **whole-wheat flour**
½ teaspoon **baking soda**
1 cup **rolled oats**
⅓ cup chopped **dried apricots**
¼ cup chopped **dried figs**
⅓ cup **mixed seeds**, such as pumpkin, sunflower, and sesame

Line 2 baking sheets with nonstick parchment paper.

Beat together the margarine and sugar in a bowl until light and fluffy, then beat in the egg and measured water.

Sift the flour and baking soda into the bowl, adding any bran in the sifter. Add the oats, apricots, figs, and seeds, then fold all the ingredients into the margarine and sugar mixture.

Place 24 walnut-size pieces of the dough on the baking sheets and flatten them slightly with the back of a fork.

Bake the bites in a preheated oven, at 350°F, for 10–15 minutes, until golden. Transfer to a wire rack to cool.

For citrus fig & pine nut bites, beat together the margarine and sugar, then beat in the egg and 2 tablespoons orange juice instead of the water. Combine the remaining ingredients in a bowl, as above, replacing the apricots with ¼ cup chopped citrus peel, and the mixed seeds with ⅓ cup pine nuts. Shape and cook as above.

mini orange shortbreads

Calories per shortbread **30**
Makes **80**
Preparation time **10 minutes**,
  plus cooling
Cooking time **10–12 minutes**

2 cups **all-purpose flour**,
  sifted
1 ½ sticks **unsalted butter**, cut
  into small pieces
grated zest of **1 orange**
½ teaspoon **allspice**
⅓ cup **granulated sugar**
2 teaspoons **cold water**

To serve
2 teaspoons **confectioners'
  sugar**
1 teaspoon **unsweetened
  cocoa powder**

Put the flour into a bowl, add the butter, and rub in with the fingertips until the mixture resembles fine bread crumbs. Stir in the remaining ingredients with the measured water and mix to form a dough.

Roll out the dough on a lightly floured surface to a thickness of ⅛ inch. Using a ¾ inch plain cutter, cut out about 80 circles.

Place the circles on nonstick baking sheets and bake in a preheated oven, at 400°F, for 10–12 minutes, until golden. Carefully transfer to a wire rack to cool.

Mix together the confectioners' sugar and cocoa powder and dust a little over the shortbreads before serving.

For cardamom & rosewater mini shortbreads,

crush 5 cardamom pods and pick out the seeds. Discard the pods. Grind the seeds in a mortar and pestle and put into a bowl with the flour and butter. Rub together the flour and butter as above, then add the orange, sugar, 1 ½ teaspoons cold water, and ½ teaspoon rosewater, omitting the allspice. Bring the dough together, then roll out and bake as above. Serve dusted with confectioners' sugar, omitting the cocoa powder.

cranberry & hazelnut cookies

Calories per cookie **60**
Makes **30**
Preparation time **10 minutes**
Cooking time **5–6 minutes**

4 tablespoons **unsalted
    butter**, softened, or ¼ cup
    polyunsaturated margarine
⅓ cup **granulated sugar**
2 tablespoons packed **light
    brown sugar**
1 **egg**, beaten
a few drops of **vanilla extract**
1¼ cups **all-purpose flour**,
    sifted
1¼ teaspoons **baking powder**
½ cup **rolled oats**
⅓ cup **dried cranberries**
⅓ cup **hazelnuts**, toasted
    and chopped

Line 2 baking sheets with nonstick parchment paper.

Beat together the butter, sugars, egg, and vanilla extract in a large bowl until smooth.

Stir in the flour, baking powder, and oats, then the dried cranberries and chopped hazelnuts.

Place 30 teaspoonfuls of the dough onto the baking sheets and flatten them slightly with the back of a fork.

Bake in a preheated oven, at 350°F, for 5–6 minutes, until browned. Transfer to a wire rack to cool.

For dark chocolate & ginger cookies, prepare the dough as above, omitting the cranberries and hazelnuts. Replace them with ¼ cup semisweet chocolate chips and 2 pieces of chopped preserved ginger or ½ teaspoon of peeled and grated fresh ginger root. Stir together and bake as above.

white chocolate drops

Calories per biscuit **98**
Makes **20**
Preparation time **10 minutes**,
  plus chilling and cooling
Cooking time **20 minutes**

¼ cup **vegetable shortening**
4 tablespoons **butter**,
  softened
¼ cup **granulated sugar**
1 **egg yolk**
1¼ cups **brown rice flour**
1 tablespoon **ground almonds
  (almond meal)**
2 oz **white chocolate**, grated
2 teaspoons **confectioners'
  sugar**, to serve

Put the fats and sugar into a large bowl and beat together, then beat in the egg yolk followed by the remaining ingredients. Form the dough into a ball, wrap closely in plastic wrap, and chill for 1 hour.

Remove the dough from the refrigerator, unwrap, and place on a lightly floured surface. Knead the dough a little to soften it, then divide into 20 balls.

Place the balls on 2 baking sheets, flatten them slightly with a fork, and bake in a preheated oven, at 350°F, for about 20 minutes, until golden. Transfer to a wire rack to cool. Dust with a little confectioners' sugar before serving.

For chocolate & coconut bites, make the cookies as above, omitting the ground almonds. Put 2 oz semisweet chocolate into a heatproof bowl and melt over a saucepan of gently simmering water. Dip one-quarter of each cooled cookie in the chocolate, then dip the chocolate-coated edge of the cookies in ¾ cup unsweetened dried coconut. Place on a tray in the refrigerator for 20 minutes to let the chocolate set, then store the cookies in an airtight container. There will be plenty of leftover chocolate and coconut, but you will need this quantity so that the job of dipping the cookies is not too difficult.

orange & cornmeal cookies

Calories per cookie **67**
Makes **20**
Preparation time **10 minutes**,
  plus chilling
Cooking time **8 minutes**

½ cup **cornmeal**
2½ tablespoons **rice flour**
¼ cup **ground almonds**
  (almond meal)
½ teaspoon **baking powder**
⅔ cup **confectioners' sugar**
4 tablespoons **butter**, cubed
1 **egg yolk**, beaten
grated zest **1 orange**
¼ cup **slivered almonds**

Line 2 baking sheets with nonstick parchment paper. Put the cornmeal, flour, ground almonds, baking powder, confectioners' sugar, and butter in a food processor and blend until the mixture resembles fine bread crumbs, or rub in by hand in a large bowl.

Stir in the egg yolk and orange zest and bring together to make a dough. Wrap closely in plastic wrap and chill for 30 minutes.

Remove the dough from the refrigerator, unwrap, and roll out thinly on a lightly floured surface. Cut into 20 circles with a 1½ inch cutter. Transfer to the prepared baking sheets, sprinkle with the slivered almonds, and bake in a preheated oven, at 350°F, for about 8 minutes, until golden. Let the cookies cool on the sheets for a few minutes to harden, then transfer to a wire rack to cool.

For Christmasy cornmeal cookies, prepare the dough as above, adding ¼ teaspoon vanilla extract and ½ teaspoon each of ground cinnamon and allspice when stirring in the egg. Chill and roll out as above, then use a star-shape cookie cutter to cut out the cookies. Place on baking sheets lined with nonstick parchment paper and cook as above, omitting the slivered almonds.

lemon, pistachio & date squares

Calories per square **174**
Makes **20**
Preparation time **10 minutes**,
  plus cooling and chilling
Cooking time **20 minutes**

grated zest of 1 **lemon**
⅔ cup chopped **dried dates**
⅔ cup **unsalted pistachio
  nuts**, chopped
¾ cup **slivered almonds**,
  chopped
½ cup firmly packed **light
  brown sugar**
1½ cups **millet flakes**
1½ cups **cornflakes**,
  lightly crushed
1 (14 oz) can **low-fat
  condensed milk**
2–3 tablespoons **mixed
  seeds**, such as pumpkin
  and sunflower

Simply put all the ingredients into a large bowl and mix together. Spoon into an 11 x 7 inch baking pan and spread evenly. Bake in a preheated oven, at 350°F, for 20 minutes.

Let cool in the pan, then mark into 20 squares and chill until firm.

For chocolate & almond squares, make the batter as above, omitting the pistachios and slivered almonds. Coarsely chop 1 cup blanched almonds and add to the mixture with 1⅔ cups bran flakes and 2 oz melted semisweet chocolate. Cook and cool, mark, and chill as above, drizzling the top with melted white chocolate once cooled, if desired.

passion cake squares

Calories per square **307**
Makes **16**
Preparation time **10 minutes**,
  plus cooling
Cooking time **1 hour**

1 cup **brown rice flour**
1¾ cups **granulated sugar**
2 teaspoons **baking powder**
1 teaspoon **xanthan gum**
1 teaspoon **ground cinnamon**
⅔ cup **canola** or **corn oil**
2 **eggs**, beaten
a few drops of **vanilla extract**
3⅓ cups shredded **carrots**
¾ cup **unsweetened
  dried coconut**
½ cup drained **canned
  crushed pineapple**
⅓ cup **golden raisins**

Topping
1 cup **low-fat cream cheese**
2 tablespoons **honey**
¾ cup **walnuts**, chopped
  (optional)

Grease and flour an 8 inch square cake pan. Sift the flour, sugar, baking powder, xanthan gum, and cinnamon into a large bowl. Add the oil, eggs, and vanilla extract and beat well.

Fold in the carrots, coconut, pineapple, and golden raisins and spoon the batter into the prepared pan. Bake in a preheated oven, at 350°F, for about 1 hour or until a toothpick inserted in the middle comes out clean. Let cool in the pan.

Beat together the cream cheese and honey and smooth over the cake, then sprinkle the nuts, if using, on top. Cut into 16 squares.

For tropical cake squares, prepare the cake batter as in the first step above, omitting the cinnamon. Peel and pit 1 small ripe mango and coarsely chop it. Fold it into the batter with the carrots, coconut, and ½ cup chopped Brazil nuts. Omit the pineapple and golden raisins. Bake and cool as above. For the topping, fold the flesh of 3 passion fruits into the cream cheese, sweeten with honey to taste, then spread over the cake. Cut into squares, omitting the walnuts.

moist banana & carrot cake

Calories per serving **183**
Serves **14**
Preparation time **10 minutes**,
   plus cooling
Cooking time **1 hour**
   40 minutes

1⅓ cups coarsely chopped
   dried apricots
½ cup **water**
1 **egg**
2 tablespoons **honey**
1 cup coarsely chopped
   walnuts
4 ripe **bananas**, mashed
1 large **carrot**, shredded
1¾ cups **all-purpose flour**,
   sifted
1¾ teaspoons **baking powder**

Topping
⅔ cup **low-fat cream cheese**
2 tablespoons **lemon curd**

Grease and line a 9 x 5 x 3 inch loaf pan. Put the apricots into a small saucepan with the measured water, bring to a boil, then reduce the heat and simmer for 10 minutes. Transfer to a blender or food processor and blend to form a thick puree.

Put all the remaining cake ingredients in a large bowl and add the apricot puree. Mix well, then spoon into the pan.

Bake in a preheated oven, at 350°F, for 1½ hours or until a toothpick inserted in the middle comes out clean. Turn out onto a wire rack to cool.

Beat together the cream cheese and lemon curd in a bowl, then spread over the top of the cooled loaf. Serve cut into 14 slices.

For date & banana cake, replace the apricots with 1 cup pitted dates. Cook and puree as above, reducing the water to ⅓ cup. Make the cake batter with all the above ingredients, using the date puree instead of the apricot and adding 2 teaspoons allspice. Bake and let cool as above. Combine 1 teaspoon ground cinnamon with 2 tablespoons granulated sugar and dust over the cake instead of the lemon topping.

chocolate, zucchini & nut cake

Calories per serving **237**
Serves **12**
Preparation time **10 minutes**,
  plus cooling
Cooking time **40 minutes**

2 cups shredded **zucchini**
2 **eggs**
½ cup **vegetable oil**
grated zest and juice of
  1 **orange**
⅔ cup **granulated sugar**
1¾ cups **all-purpose flour**
2 tablespoons **unsweetened**
  cocoa powder
½ teaspoon **baking soda**
2¼ teaspoons **baking powder**
⅓ cup chopped **dried**
  apricots

Topping
1 cup **low-fat cream cheese**
2 tablespoons **chocolate**
  hazelnut spread
1 tablespoon **hazelnuts**,
  toasted and chopped

Grease and line a deep 8 inch loose-bottom cake pan. Put the zucchini into a strainer and squeeze out any excess liquid.

Beat together the eggs, vegetable oil, orange zest and juice, and sugar in a large bowl. Sift in the flour, cocoa powder, baking soda, and baking powder and beat to combine.

Fold in the zucchini and apricots, then spoon the batter into the prepared pan.

Bake in a preheated oven, at 350°F, for 40 minutes, until risen and firm to the touch. Turn out onto a wire rack to cool.

Beat together the cream cheese and chocolate hazelnut spread in a bowl, then spread over the top of the cake. Sprinkle with the hazelnuts and serve cut into 12 slices.

For strawberry & ricotta topping, to use instead of the chocolate and hazelnut topping, blend ⅔ cup hulled strawberries in a blender or food processor with 1 tablespoon honey to make a puree. Stir in ½ cup fat-free ricotta and spread over the top of the cooled cake. Decorate the top of the cake with halved strawberries, if desired.

olive & haloumi bread

Calories per serving **189**
Serves **12**
Preparation time **15 minutes**,
  plus proving
Cooking time **35 minutes**

3⅔ cups **strong all-purpose
  flour**, plus extra for sifting
2¼ teaspoons (1 envelope)
  active dry yeast
pinch of **salt**
2 tablespoons **olive oil**
1¼ cups **warm water**
1 **onion**, thinly sliced
1 cup **pitted olives**
3 oz **low-fat haloumi, feta,**
  or **mozzarella cheese**,
  chopped
2 tablespoons chopped
  parsley

Put the flour, yeast, and salt into a large bowl. Combine half the oil with the measured water in a small bowl and stir into the flour to form a dough.

Turn the dough out onto a lightly floured surface and knead for 5 minutes, until smooth and elastic. Place in a lightly oiled bowl, cover with a damp cloth, and set aside in a warm place for about 1 hour, until doubled in size.

Meanwhile, heat the remaining oil in a skillet, add the onion, and sauté for 7–8 minutes, until softened and golden. Let cool.

Turn the risen dough out onto the floured surface and add the remaining ingredients, including the onion, kneading it into the dough. Shape into an oval, place on a lightly floured baking sheet, and let rise for 1 hour.

When the loaf has risen, slash a few cuts in the top, sift over a little flour, then bake in a preheated oven, at 425°F, for about 25 minutes, until hollow-sounding when tapped. Transfer to a wire rack to cool.

For olive & sun-dried tomato swirls, make the dough and let rise until doubled in size. Sauté the onions in the oil as above, then stir in the olives, ½ cup chopped sun-dried tomatoes, and ½ teaspoon fennel seeds and let cool. Roll the dough out on a floured surface to about 8 x 11 inches and spread with the olive, onion, and tomato mixture. Roll up the dough from one long end and cut the roll into 12 circles. Lay them on a large baking sheet dusted with flour, cover with a damp cloth, and let rise for 30 minutes. Bake in a preheated oven, at 425°F, for 12–15 minutes, until golden.

feta & herb loaf

Calories per serving **118**
Serves **14**
Preparation time **10 minutes**,
    plus proving
Cooking time **45 minutes**

1 ½ cups **cornmeal**
⅔ cup **rice flour**
¾ cup **instant dry milk**
pinch of **salt**
2¼ teaspoons (1 envelope)
    acitve dry yeast
2 teaspoons **granulated
    sugar**
2 teaspoons **xanthan gum**
3 **eggs**, beaten
2 tablespoons chopped
    mixed herbs
2 cups **tepid water**
⅔ cup crumbled **feta cheese**

Grease and line a 9 x 5 x 3 inch loaf pan. Sift the cornmeal, flour, dry milk, and salt into a large bowl and stir well to combine. Stir in the yeast, sugar, and xanthan gum.

Put the eggs, herbs, and measured water into a bowl and mix together. Stir this mixture into the dry ingredients and combine to form a soft dough. Beat for 5 minutes, then stir in the feta cheese.

Spoon the dough into the prepared pan, cover with a clean damp kitchen towel, and let rest in a warm place to rise for about 30 minutes, until the dough is near the top of the pan. Bake in a preheated oven, at 350°F, for about 45 minutes, until brown and hollow-sounding when tapped. Transfer to a wire rack to cool.

For cornmeal, spinach & chile loaf, make the dough as above, replacing the feta cheese with ½ cup cooked spinach (squeezed dry in a kitchen towel, then finely chopped), 1 teaspoon caraway seeds, and 1 seeded and finely chopped red chile. Let rise in the pan, bake, and cool as above.

nutty seed loaf

Calories per serving **263**
Serves **8**
Preparation time **10 minutes**
Cooking time **25 minutes**

2½ cups **brown rice flour**,
  plus extra for sifting
¼ cup **rice bran**
2 tablespoons **instant
  dry milk**
½ teaspoon **baking soda**
1 teaspoon **baking powder**
½–1 teaspoon **salt**
1 teaspoon **xanthan gum**
pinch of **granulated sugar**
⅓ cup **mixed seeds**, such as
  sunflower and pumpkin
½ cup **hazelnuts**, toasted and
  coarsely chopped
1 **egg**, lightly beaten
1¼ cups **buttermilk**

Put all the dry ingredients into a large bowl and mix together. In a separate bowl, mix together the egg and buttermilk, then stir into the dry ingredients.

Turn the dough out onto a lightly floured surface and form into a circle about 8 inches in diameter. Mark into 8 segments, then place on a baking sheet and sift a little extra flour over it.

Place in an oven preheated to its highest setting and cook for 10 minutes, then reduce the heat to 400°F, and continue to cook for about 15 minutes, until golden and sounding hollow when tapped. Transfer to a wire rack to cool.

For seeded Parmesan rolls, make the dough as above, using ⅓ cup sesame seeds instead of the mixed seeds, and replacing the hazelnuts with ½ cup grated Parmesan cheese. Shape the dough into 8 round rolls, then place on a baking sheet and dust with a little extra flour. Bake for 10 minutes as above, then reduce the oven heat as above and cook for another 8–10 minutes, until the rolls sound hollow when tapped.

index

acknowledgments

Recipe Consultant: Angela Dowden
Commissioning Editor: Eleanor Maxfield
Senior Editor: Leanne Bryan
Designer: Eoghan O'Brien
Design: Jeremy Tilston
Picture Library Manager: Jen Veall
Production Controller: Sarah Kramer

Picture Acknowledgments
Octopus Publishing Group Stephen Conroy 10, 59, 61,
67, 89, 145, 147, 161, 163; Will Heap 164/165; David
Munns 46/47; Emma Neish 175, 201, 207, 209, 211,
221, 223, 225, 233, 235; Lis Parsons 1, 15, 16, 17,
21, 25, 81, 87, 93, 107, 109, 113, 125, 131, 137, 141,
143, 155, 157, 159, 167, 171, 179, 181, 185, 197, 203,
213, 217, 227, 229, 231; William Reavell 4/5, 33, 103,
115, 133; Craig Robertson 29, 37, 39, 51, 97; Gareth
Sambidge 9, 63, 193; William Shaw 2/3, 6/7, 12, 23, 27,
31, 35, 41, 43, 45, 49, 53, 55, 57, 65, 69, 71, 73, 75, 77,
79, 83, 85, 91, 95, 111, 117, 121, 123, 127, 135, 139,
149, 151, 153, 169, 173, 177, 183, 187, 189, 191, 195,
205, 215, 219; Eleanor Skan 13; Simon Smith 99, 101,
119, 129; Ian Wallace 18/19, 104/105, 198/199.